Empowering Indian Women

-A Woman's Guide to Financial Freedom in Today's World

By Shikha RVN Kaushik

Index

Preface

In a world that is rapidly evolving, the role of women, especially in India, has been undergoing a profound transformation. Today, women are not just homemakers; they are leaders, entrepreneurs, professionals, and decision-makers. They are breaking barriers, shattering stereotypes, and carving out spaces for themselves in every sector of society. Yet, despite these strides, one critical aspect remains a challenge for many women: financial independence.

This book, "Empowering Indian Women: A Journey to Financial Independence," is born out of a deep-seated belief that financial independence is not just a luxury, but a necessity. It is the foundation upon which women can build their dreams, protect their futures, and contribute meaningfully to their families and communities. Financial independence is a tool of empowerment that enables women to live with dignity, make informed decisions, and pursue their passions without the fear of economic constraints.

As an author with a passion for financial literacy and women's empowerment, I have observed that the lack of financial awareness often holds women back from achieving their full potential. This book is a humble attempt to bridge that gap. It is a guide, a mentor, and a companion on the journey to financial freedom. Whether you are just starting out on your financial journey or are looking to deepen your understanding, this book is designed to offer you the knowledge, tools, and confidence to take control of your financial future.

In writing this book, I have drawn from my own experiences, the stories of countless women I have encountered, and the wisdom of financial experts. The book is structured to be practical and accessible, with step-by-step guidance on everything from budgeting and saving to investing and managing debt. Each chapter is crafted with the unique challenges and aspirations of Indian women in mind, acknowledging the cultural, societal, and economic contexts that shape our lives.

But beyond the practical advice, this book is also a celebration of the power of women. It is a tribute to the resilience, creativity, and strength that women display every day in managing their households, raising their children, and pursuing their careers. It is a reminder that financial independence is not just about money; it is about empowerment, freedom, and the ability to live life on your own terms.

As you embark on this journey through the pages of this book, I encourage you to approach it with an open mind and a willingness to take action. Financial independence is a journey, not a destination. It requires discipline, determination, and a commitment to learning and growing. But it is a journey worth taking, and I am honored to be your guide.

Thank you for choosing this book as your companion on this journey. I hope it inspires you, empowers you, and helps you to achieve the financial freedom you deserve.

Warm regards,

Shikha Kaushik

Chapter 1
Introduction - The Power of Financial Independence

In the vibrant and diverse landscape of India, the role of women is evolving rapidly. From bustling urban centers to serene rural areas, women are making their mark in every field, breaking barriers and shattering glass ceilings. Yet, despite these strides, one crucial aspect often remains overlooked: financial independence.

Financial independence is not just about having money in the bank; it's about having the freedom to make choices that shape your life. It's about the confidence that comes from knowing you can support yourself and your loved ones, pursue your dreams, and navigate life's challenges without relying on others. For Indian women, this concept carries profound significance, given the unique socio-cultural dynamics we navigate daily.

Growing up in India, many of us have been taught the virtues of managing a household, but discussions around managing finances are often reserved for the men in our lives. This traditional mindset can hinder our ability to fully realize our potential. Financial independence empowers us to take control of our destiny, break free from restrictive norms, and live life on our terms.

Consider the stories of inspiring Indian women who have embraced financial independence. From entrepreneurs like Falguni Nayar, founder of Nykaa, to leaders like Kiran Mazumdar-Shaw of Biocon, these women have not only achieved personal success but have also become beacons of hope and role models for countless others. Their journeys underline a vital truth: financial empowerment can be a game-changer, enabling women to transform their lives and their communities.

Financial independence offers more than just economic stability; it provides emotional and psychological strength. When you are financially independent, you can make decisions based on your values and aspirations rather than out of necessity. You gain the confidence to leave unhealthy relationships, invest in your education, start a business, or support your family in meaningful ways. It's about having a voice and the means to ensure it is heard.

In the Indian context, where family and community ties are strong, achieving financial independence also means contributing to the well-being of those around you. It means being able to support your parents in their old age, providing quality education for your children, and ensuring a better quality of life for your family. It's about breaking the cycle of dependence and setting a new precedent for the next generation.

The journey to financial independence is not without its challenges. Societal expectations, gender biases, and economic barriers can make this path seem daunting. However, with determination, education, and the right strategies, it is entirely achievable. This book aims to be your guide, offering practical advice and insights tailored to the unique experiences of Indian women.

As you embark on this journey, remember that financial independence is not a destination but a continuous process of growth and learning. It's about making informed decisions, taking calculated risks, and constantly adapting to changing circumstances. Whether you are just starting out in your career, looking to advance, or planning for retirement, every step you take towards financial independence is a step towards a more empowered and fulfilling life.

In the chapters that follow, we will explore the foundations of financial independence, delve into practical strategies for earning, saving, and investing, and address the unique challenges you may face along the way. Together, we will uncover the power that comes from financial freedom and how it can transform not just your life, but the lives of those around you.

So, let's begin this journey with the understanding that financial independence is not just about wealth—it's about freedom, empowerment, and the ability to live life on your own terms. Welcome to the path of financial empowerment. Welcome to a future where you are in control.

<u>Understanding Financial Independence</u>

Financial independence is a term that often gets thrown around, but what does it truly mean, especially for women in India? At its core, financial independence is about having the ability to support yourself without relying on others. It means having enough resources to cover your needs and wants, allowing you to make choices that align with your values and aspirations.

<u>Defining Financial Independence</u>

Financial independence is not just about earning a high income or accumulating wealth. It's about having control over your finances and making informed decisions that enable you to live a comfortable and secure life. For Indian women, financial independence can mean different things at various stages of life. It could be the freedom to pursue higher education, start a business, travel, or provide for your family. It's about having the means to make choices that enhance your quality of life.

<u>The Importance of Financial Independence for Women</u>

1. **Empowerment and Confidence**: Financial independence boosts your confidence and self-worth. When you can support yourself, you gain a sense of empowerment that permeates every aspect of your life. This confidence allows you to assert your opinions, make decisions, and take control of your future.

2. **Freedom from Dependence**: Traditionally, many Indian women have been financially dependent on their parents, spouses, or other family members. This dependence can limit your choices and make you vulnerable to control or abuse. Financial independence provides the freedom to make decisions that are best for you without being influenced by financial constraints.

3. **Ability to Pursue Dreams**: Whether it's starting a business, traveling, or pursuing higher education, financial independence gives you the freedom to chase your dreams. You can invest in yourself and your aspirations without worrying about financial limitations.

4. **Security and Stability**: Life is unpredictable, and having financial independence ensures that you are prepared for any unforeseen circumstances. It provides a safety net that can help you navigate through difficult times, such as job loss, illness, or other emergencies.

5. **Impact on Family and Community**: Financially independent women are in a better position to support their families and contribute to their communities. You can provide better education and opportunities for your children, support your parents, and contribute to the economic growth of your community.

Barriers to Financial Independence

Achieving financial independence is not without its challenges, especially in a diverse and complex society like India. Here are some common barriers women face:

1. **Societal Expectations and Norms**: Traditional gender roles often dictate that men are the primary breadwinners, while women manage the household. These societal expectations can limit women's opportunities for education and employment.

2. **Gender Pay Gap**: Despite progress, women often earn less than men for the same work. This wage disparity can make it harder for women to achieve financial independence.

3. **Limited Access to Education and Employment**: In many parts of India, girls and women still face barriers to accessing quality education and employment opportunities. These barriers can limit their ability to become financially independent.

4. **Lack of Financial Literacy**: Financial education is crucial for managing money effectively, yet many women lack the necessary knowledge and skills. This lack of financial literacy can hinder their ability to save, invest, and plan for the future.

Overcoming the Barriers

While these challenges are significant, they are not insurmountable. Here are some strategies to overcome them:

1. **Education and Skill Development**: Invest in your education and acquire skills that are in demand in the job market. Continuous learning and professional development can enhance your career prospects and earning potential.

2. **Financial Literacy**: Educate yourself about financial management, savings, investments, and budgeting. Understanding how to manage money is crucial for achieving financial independence.

3. **Networking and Mentorship**: Connect with other women who are financially independent and seek mentorship. Learn from their experiences and gain insights into navigating financial challenges.

4. **Advocacy and Support:** Advocate for gender equality and support initiatives that promote women's education and employment. Collective efforts can bring about positive change in society.

Financial independence is a journey, and every step you take brings you closer to achieving it. In the following chapters, we will explore practical strategies and tips to help you on this journey. Remember, financial independence is not just a goal; it's a path to empowerment, freedom, and a better future for yourself and those around you. Let's embark on this journey together and unlock the power of financial independence.

Why Financial Freedom Matters for Women Today

Financial freedom is crucial for everyone, but it holds particular significance for women in today's world, especially in India. Here's why:

1. Empowerment and Self-Reliance

Financial freedom is a powerful tool for empowerment. It enables women to make choices based on their preferences and values, rather than out of necessity. When women are financially independent, they can pursue careers, education, and personal growth without relying on others. This self-reliance fosters confidence and a sense of control over their lives.

2. Breaking Free from Traditional Roles

In many Indian families, traditional gender roles still dominate. Women are often expected to prioritize household responsibilities and caregiving over personal and professional growth. Financial independence allows women to challenge and break free from these restrictive norms, enabling them to pursue their aspirations and contribute to society in diverse ways.

3. Enhancing Decision-Making Power

Financial freedom significantly enhances a woman's decision-making power within her family and community. When women contribute financially, they gain a stronger voice in matters such as household finances, children's education, and healthcare decisions. This shift in dynamics promotes equality and respect within the family structure.

4. Ensuring Personal Safety and Security

Financial independence is also a key factor in ensuring personal safety and security. Women who are financially stable have the means to leave abusive or unhealthy relationships. They can secure safe housing, seek legal assistance, and rebuild their lives without fear of financial instability. This autonomy is critical for their physical and emotional well-being.

5. Pursuing Dreams and Ambitions

Financial freedom provides the resources necessary to pursue dreams and ambitions. Whether it's starting a business, traveling, or investing in further education, financial independence makes these goals achievable. Women can take risks, innovate, and explore new opportunities without being hindered by financial constraints.

6. Contributing to Economic Growth

When women achieve financial independence, they contribute significantly to the economy. Increased participation of women in the workforce leads to higher productivity, innovation, and economic growth. Women's financial contributions support their families and communities, creating a positive ripple effect throughout society.

7. Providing for the Next Generation

Financially independent women are better equipped to provide for their children and ensure their future success. They can afford quality education, healthcare, and extracurricular activities that contribute to their children's overall development. By modeling financial independence, women also inspire the next generation to value and pursue economic self-sufficiency.

8. Navigating Life's Challenges

Life is full of uncertainties, and financial independence provides a safety net to navigate these challenges. Whether it's a medical emergency, job loss, or a sudden family crisis, having financial resources allows women to manage and overcome these situations with resilience and stability. It reduces anxiety and stress, ensuring a more secure future.

9. Combating Societal Inequities

Financial freedom helps combat societal inequities by reducing the gender pay gap and promoting equal opportunities. When women are financially independent, they can advocate for fair treatment, equal pay, and workplace diversity. This progress contributes to a more just and equitable society for everyone.

10. Building a Legacy

Finally, financial independence enables women to build a legacy. They can create wealth that benefits future generations, support charitable causes, and invest in initiatives that reflect their values. This legacy is not just about money; it's about the impact and influence they leave behind, shaping a better world for others.

Conclusion

Financial freedom is not just about having money; it's about having the power to shape your own life and contribute meaningfully to society. For Indian women, achieving financial independence is a transformative journey that empowers them to break free from traditional constraints, enhance their decision-making power, and ensure personal and familial security.

As we continue this journey through the book, we will explore practical steps and strategies to achieve financial independence. Remember, financial freedom is within your reach, and it holds the key to unlocking your true potential and living a life of empowerment, purpose, and fulfillment.

Chapter 2
The Landscape: Challenges Women Face

The journey towards financial independence for women in India is both inspiring and challenging. Understanding the landscape, they navigate helps us appreciate the progress made and the barriers that still exist. This section will provide an overview of the key challenges Indian women face as they strive for financial independence, setting the stage for deeper discussions in the following sections.

Indian women have made remarkable strides in education, entrepreneurship, and leadership. However, they still confront significant obstacles that can hinder their financial autonomy. These challenges are multifaceted, stemming from historical contexts, societal norms, economic disparities, and cultural expectations.

Educational Barriers

Access to education has improved, but disparities remain. In rural areas, girls often have less access to quality education compared to their urban counterparts. Economic constraints, gender biases, and safety concerns can all contribute to higher dropout rates among girls.

Example: Asha, a girl from a remote village in Bihar, had to walk several kilometers to reach the nearest school. Despite her enthusiasm for learning, her parents prioritized her brothers' education, considering it a better investment. A local NGO intervened, providing transportation and scholarships that enabled Asha to continue her education. She later became a teacher, advocating for girls' education in her community.

Employment Challenges

Women entering the workforce face hurdles such as discrimination, lack of opportunities, and workplace harassment. Even when employed, they are often underrepresented in higher-paying and leadership roles, limiting their financial growth.

Example: Rina, an MBA graduate from Kolkata, struggled to find a job that matched her qualifications. She encountered gender biases during interviews and was often offered lower positions than her male peers. Refusing to be disheartened, Rina started her own consulting firm, creating jobs for other women and proving that talent and determination can break barriers.

Societal Expectations

Traditional gender roles and societal expectations often dictate that women prioritize family over career. This dual burden can hinder professional growth and limit their ability to achieve financial independence.

Example: Leela, a successful IT professional in Bangalore, faced criticism for hiring domestic help to manage household chores. Balancing her demanding job and family responsibilities, she challenged the notion that women must do it all without support. Her decision to seek help allowed her to excel at work and maintain a healthy work-life balance, setting an example for others.

Gender Pay Gap

The gender pay gap is a persistent issue, with women earning less than men for the same work. This disparity affects their immediate financial stability and long-term economic security.

Example: Suman, a graphic designer in Delhi, discovered that her male colleagues were earning significantly more for similar roles. She educated herself about salary negotiation and advocated for pay transparency in her organization. Her efforts resulted in a raise and initiated company-wide changes towards pay equity.

Cultural Barriers

Cultural norms can restrict women's financial autonomy. In some communities, women are discouraged from managing finances or having their own bank accounts, perpetuating financial dependence on male family members.

Example: Parvati, from a traditional family in Tamil Nadu, was not allowed to handle money independently. After attending a financial literacy workshop, she gained the confidence and skills to start a small business. Her success not only provided financial security for her family but also inspired other women in her community to take control of their finances.

The landscape of financial independence for Indian women is complex and challenging, shaped by educational barriers, employment challenges, societal expectations, the gender pay gap, and cultural norms. Despite these obstacles, countless women are making strides towards financial autonomy, breaking barriers, and inspiring others along the way.

As we move forward, we will explore the historical context and progress that have shaped this landscape. Understanding the past helps us appreciate the journey and recognize the importance of continued efforts towards achieving financial independence for all women in India.

Historical Context and Progress

Understanding the historical context of women's financial independence in India provides insight into the significant strides made and the persistent challenges that remain. The journey of Indian women toward financial autonomy is marked by both societal constraints and remarkable achievements.

Historical Context

Traditionally, Indian society was predominantly patriarchal, with women confined to domestic roles. Education and employment opportunities for women were limited, and their financial decisions were typically controlled by male family members. This cultural setup meant that women's financial independence was virtually nonexistent.

Example: In the early 20th century, women like Kamala Devi Chattopadhyay began challenging these norms. As a freedom fighter and social reformer, Kamala Devi played a crucial role in advocating for women's rights, including their economic empowerment. Her efforts laid the groundwork for future generations of women to seek financial independence.

Progress Over the Decades

The post-independence era marked the beginning of significant changes. Government policies and social movements aimed at empowering women brought about gradual improvements in their status. Key milestones include:

1. 1950s-1960s: The Indian constitution granted equal rights to men and women. Educational institutions started admitting more women, and laws were enacted to protect women's rights.

2. 1970s-1980s: The women's movement gained momentum, addressing issues such as dowry, domestic violence, and workplace discrimination. This period also saw an increase in women entering the workforce, particularly in urban areas.

3. 1990s-Present: Economic liberalization and globalization opened new opportunities for women. The IT and service sectors provided employment to a large number of educated women. Initiatives like the Self-Help Group (SHG) movement empowered rural women by providing them with microfinance and entrepreneurial opportunities.

Example: Kiran Mazumdar-Shaw, who founded Biocon in 1978, is a notable example of progress. Starting with limited resources, she built Biocon into one of India's leading biotechnology companies. Kiran's journey reflects the broader trend of women breaking barriers in traditionally male-dominated fields.

Government Initiatives

Several government schemes and policies have been implemented to promote women's financial independence. These include:

1. **Beti Bachao Beti Padhao** (Save the daughter, Educate the daughter): Launched in 2015, this campaign aims to address gender discrimination and promote education for girls.

2. **Stand-Up India Scheme:** This initiative provides loans to women entrepreneurs to encourage them to start their own businesses.

3. **Mahila E-Haat:** An online platform to support women entrepreneurs by providing them with market access.

Example: Nisha, a beneficiary of the Stand-Up India Scheme, used the loan to start a tailoring business in her village. The financial support helped her expand her business, employ other women, and achieve economic stability for her family. Her success story is an inspiration for many women in her community.

Changing Social Attitudes

Societal attitudes toward women's roles have also evolved. There is greater acceptance of women pursuing higher education and careers. Media and popular culture have played a significant role in shaping these attitudes by showcasing empowered female characters and highlighting women's achievements.

Example: The success of movies like Dangal, which tells the story of female wrestlers Geeta and Babita Phogat, has contributed to changing perceptions about women in sports and other non-traditional fields. Their story not only inspired many young girls to take up sports but also highlighted the importance of family support in achieving one's dreams.

Conclusion

The historical context of women's financial independence in India is a tapestry of struggle and triumph. From traditional constraints to modern-day achievements, the journey reflects the resilience and determination of Indian women. While significant progress has been made, there is still a long way to go.

As we continue to explore the challenges and opportunities, it is crucial to build on the progress made and address the persistent barriers that hinder women's financial independence. In the next section, we will delve into the issue of the gender pay gap, examining its impact and exploring strategies to overcome it.

Gender Pay Gap

One of the most persistent and pervasive challenges facing women in their pursuit of financial independence is the gender pay gap. Despite significant advancements in education and employment, women in India continue to earn less than their male counterparts for the same work. This disparity not only affects women's immediate financial stability but also has long-term implications for their economic security and overall well-being.

Understanding the Gender Pay Gap

The gender pay gap refers to the difference in earnings between men and women. This gap can be measured in various ways, including hourly wages, monthly salaries, and overall earnings. In India, the gender pay gap is influenced by a range of factors, including occupational segregation, discrimination, and differences in work experience and education.

Example: Anita, a software developer in Hyderabad, discovered that she was being paid significantly less than her male colleagues with similar experience and responsibilities. Despite her high performance and dedication, Anita's salary lagged behind. This experience is not uncommon, as women in many industries face similar disparities in pay.

Factors Contributing to the Gender Pay Gap

1. **Occupational Segregation**: Women are often concentrated in lower-paying jobs and industries. Even within the same industry, women are less likely to hold senior or high-paying positions. This segregation can be attributed to both societal norms and structural barriers that limit women's access to certain fields.

Example: In the healthcare sector, women are predominantly found in nursing and administrative roles, which tend to be lower-paying compared to medical and executive positions typically dominated by men.

2. **Discrimination**: Gender bias and discrimination play a significant role in perpetuating the pay gap. Women may be offered lower starting salaries than men, receive smaller raises, and be overlooked for promotions. This discrimination can be both overt and subtle, making it challenging to address.

Example: Pooja, an MBA graduate, noticed that during campus placements, male candidates were often offered higher starting salaries and more prestigious roles compared to female candidates with similar qualifications.

3. **Work Experience and Education**: Women often take career breaks for caregiving responsibilities, leading to gaps in work experience. Additionally, societal expectations may discourage women from pursuing advanced education or professional development, limiting their earning potential.

Example: Shalini, a marketing manager, took a two-year break from her career to care for her young children. Upon returning to work, she found it difficult to catch up with her male colleagues who had continued to advance in their careers.

4. **Negotiation and Advocacy**: Women are often less likely to negotiate their salaries compared to men. This can result from a lack of confidence, fear of backlash, or cultural conditioning that discourages assertiveness in women.

Example: Naina, a recent graduate, accepted her first job offer without negotiating her salary. She later learned that her male peers had successfully negotiated higher starting salaries, highlighting the importance of salary negotiation skills.

Impact of the Gender Pay Gap

The gender pay gap has far-reaching consequences for women's financial independence and overall economic well-being. Some of the key impacts include:

1. Reduced Lifetime Earnings: The cumulative effect of lower pay throughout a woman's career results in significantly reduced lifetime earnings. This affects their ability to save, invest, and secure a comfortable retirement.

2. Economic Vulnerability: Lower earnings make women more vulnerable to economic shocks and financial instability. It limits their ability to build emergency savings, invest in assets, and achieve long-term financial goals.

3. Limited Career Growth: The pay gap can discourage women from pursuing higher-paying roles or career advancements, perpetuating a cycle of lower earnings and limited opportunities.

4. Widening Wealth Gap: The gender pay gap contributes to the overall wealth gap between men and women. Women are less likely to accumulate wealth, making it harder to achieve financial independence and security.

Strategies to Overcome the Gender Pay Gap

Addressing the gender pay gap requires a multifaceted approach involving policy changes, organizational commitment, and individual action. Here are some strategies to bridge the gap:

1. **Equal Pay Legislation**: Strengthening and enforcing equal pay laws can help ensure that women receive fair compensation for their work. Governments and organizations must be held accountable for closing the pay gap.

2. **Transparency in Pay**: Encouraging transparency in pay practices can help identify and address disparities. Organizations should regularly review and publish pay data to promote accountability and fairness.

3. **Salary Negotiation Training**: Providing training on salary negotiation skills can empower women to advocate for fair pay. Encouraging women to confidently negotiate their salaries can help close the initial pay gap and set a precedent for future earnings.

4. **Support for Career Development**: Offering mentorship, sponsorship, and professional development opportunities can help women advance in their careers. Organizations should create pathways for women to move into higher-paying and leadership roles.

5. **Flexible Work Policies**: Implementing policies that support work-life balance, such as flexible working hours and parental leave, can help women maintain their careers without sacrificing earnings.

Example: Aarti, an HR manager, introduced a mentorship program in her company to support women's career growth. This program paired junior female employees with senior leaders who provided guidance on career advancement and salary negotiation. As a result, more women in the organization received promotions and pay raises, contributing to a more equitable workplace.

Conclusion

The gender pay gap remains a significant barrier to women's financial independence in India. By understanding the factors contributing to this disparity and implementing strategies to address it, we can work towards a more equitable and empowered future for women.

In the next section, we will explore the societal and cultural barriers that further complicate the landscape of financial independence for women in India. Understanding these barriers is crucial for developing effective solutions and fostering a supportive environment for women's economic empowerment.

Societal and Cultural Barriers

While progress has been made in advancing women's financial independence in India, societal and cultural barriers continue to pose significant challenges. These barriers are deeply ingrained in traditional beliefs, practices, and expectations that shape the roles and opportunities available to women. Overcoming these obstacles requires a concerted effort to change mindsets and promote gender equality.

Societal Expectations and Gender Roles

In many Indian communities, traditional gender roles dictate that women prioritize family responsibilities over professional ambitions. This expectation can limit women's opportunities for education and career advancement, reinforcing a cycle of financial dependency.

Example: Geeta, a talented engineer from a conservative family in Rajasthan, faced pressure to marry and prioritize household duties over her career. Despite her desire to continue working, societal expectations forced her to take a step back from her professional life. With support from her husband and in-laws, she eventually returned to work, but her career progression was significantly delayed.

Marriage and Financial Dependence

Marriage often reinforces financial dependence for women. Cultural norms typically designate men as the primary breadwinners, while women are expected to manage the household. This dynamic can limit women's financial autonomy and decision-making power.

Example: Rekha, a skilled accountant in Gujarat, was financially independent before marriage. However, after marrying, her husband's family expected her to quit her job and focus on domestic responsibilities. Rekha's struggle to maintain her financial independence highlights the cultural barriers that many married women face.

Inheritance Laws and Property Rights

Inheritance laws and property rights in India have historically favored men, limiting women's access to assets and financial resources. Although legal reforms have aimed to ensure equal rights, cultural practices often prevent women from claiming their share of inheritance.

Example: Meena, from a traditional family in Haryana, was denied her rightful share of ancestral property. Despite the legal provisions that supported her claim, family pressure and societal norms discouraged her from pursuing legal action. Meena's experience underscores the need for greater awareness and enforcement of women's property rights.

Patriarchal Mindset and Control Over Finances

A patriarchal mindset often leads to male control over family finances, restricting women's involvement in financial decisions. This control can prevent women from developing financial literacy and making independent financial choices.

Example: Savitri, a homemaker in Punjab, relied entirely on her husband for financial decisions. She had no knowledge of their family's income, savings, or investments. After her husband's sudden demise, Savitri struggled to manage the finances and secure her family's future. Her story illustrates the importance of financial literacy and independence for women.

Balancing Career and Family

The expectation that women must balance career and family without adequate support creates a significant barrier to their professional growth. Lack of access to affordable childcare, flexible work arrangements, and supportive workplaces can hinder women's ability to advance in their careers.

Example: Anjali, a marketing professional in Mumbai, found it challenging to balance her demanding job with her responsibilities as a mother. Without family support or affordable childcare options, she faced immense stress and burnout. Anjali's experience highlights the need for policies and practices that support working mothers.

Community and Peer Pressure

Community and peer pressure can also play a role in limiting women's financial independence. Women who challenge traditional norms may face criticism, isolation, and social ostracism.

Example: Radhika, an entrepreneur in Chennai, faced backlash from her community for starting her own business. Many believed that a woman's place was in the home, not in the marketplace. Despite the criticism, Radhika persevered and built a successful business, inspiring other women in her community to pursue their dreams.

Strategies to Overcome Societal and Cultural Barriers

Addressing societal and cultural barriers requires a multi-pronged approach that includes education, advocacy, and policy reforms. Here are some strategies to foster an environment that supports women's financial independence:

1. **Education and Awareness**: Promoting gender equality through education and awareness campaigns can challenge traditional norms and encourage a shift in mindset. Highlighting successful women role models can inspire change.

2. **Legal Reforms and Enforcement**: Strengthening legal frameworks that protect women's rights to inheritance, property, and employment is crucial. Ensuring that these laws are enforced and accessible can help women claim their rightful resources.

3. **Financial Literacy Programs**: Providing financial literacy programs for women can empower them to make informed financial decisions and manage their resources effectively. These programs should be tailored to address the specific needs and challenges faced by women.

4. **Supportive Workplaces**: Encouraging workplaces to adopt policies that support work-life balance, such as flexible working hours, parental leave, and childcare facilities, can help women balance their careers and family responsibilities.

5. **Community Engagement**: Engaging with community leaders and influencers to promote gender equality and challenge traditional norms can create a supportive environment for women. Community-based programs can provide women with the resources and support they need to achieve financial independence.

Example: Shikha, a social activist in West Bengal, started a community program that provided financial literacy training and support to women entrepreneurs. By engaging with local leaders and building a network of supportive peers, Shikha's program helped many women start their own businesses and achieve financial independence.

Conclusion

Societal and cultural barriers continue to impede the financial independence of women in India. By understanding these obstacles and implementing targeted strategies, we can create an environment that supports women's economic empowerment. The journey towards financial independence is challenging, but with collective effort, we can pave the way for a more equitable and prosperous future for all women.

In the next section, we will explore the delicate balance of career and family, discussing the unique challenges women face and the strategies to navigate this complex dynamic. Understanding this balance is essential for fostering an environment that supports both personal and professional growth for women.

Balancing Career and Family

For many women in India, balancing career and family responsibilities is one of the most challenging aspects of achieving financial independence. Traditional gender roles, societal expectations, and limited support systems often force women to make difficult choices between their professional ambitions and their family obligations. However, many women have found ways to navigate these challenges, creating a path that allows them to thrive both at home and in their careers.

The Dual Burden

Women are often expected to manage household duties and caregiving responsibilities in addition to their professional roles. This dual burden can lead to physical and emotional exhaustion, making it difficult for women to excel in their careers.

Example: Priya, a senior manager at a multinational company in Bangalore, struggled to balance her demanding job with her responsibilities as a mother and wife. Despite her supportive family, the societal expectation that she should be the primary caregiver created immense pressure. Priya's experience is shared by many women who juggle multiple roles every day.

Lack of Support Systems

The absence of adequate support systems, such as affordable childcare and flexible work arrangements, exacerbates the challenge of balancing career and family. Women often have to rely on family members for support, which may not always be available.

Example: Sunita, a schoolteacher in Lucknow, had to quit her job when her in-laws could no longer take care of her children. Without access to affordable daycare, she found it impossible to continue working. Sunita's story highlights the need for accessible childcare options to support working mothers.

Flexible Work Arrangements

Flexible work arrangements, such as remote work, part-time roles, and flexible hours, can help women balance their career and family responsibilities. These arrangements provide the flexibility needed to manage both professional and personal commitments effectively.

Example: Kavita, a marketing executive in Pune, benefited from her company's flexible work policy, which allowed her to work from home two days a week. This flexibility enabled her to manage her children's schedules while maintaining her professional responsibilities. Kavita's company recognized the importance of work-life balance and implemented policies to support it.

Workplace Policies and Support

Organizations that implement family-friendly policies and provide support for working parents can significantly impact women's ability to balance career and family. This includes offering parental leave, creating a supportive work environment, and promoting a culture that values work-life balance.

Example: Ananya, an HR professional in Mumbai, advocated for her company to introduce a parental leave policy that included both maternity and paternity leave. By promoting shared caregiving responsibilities, Ananya's initiative helped create a more inclusive workplace that supported both men and women in balancing their family duties.

Societal Attitudes and Expectations

Changing societal attitudes towards gender roles and expectations is crucial for supporting women in balancing career and family. Encouraging shared responsibilities at home and challenging traditional norms can create a more equitable environment.

Example: Rohit and Meera, a dual-income couple in Delhi, decided to share household and childcare responsibilities equally. By challenging traditional gender roles, they created a supportive environment that allowed both of them to pursue their careers without compromising on family time. Their approach inspired other couples in their community to adopt similar practices.

Self-Care and Time Management

Effective time management and self-care are essential for women balancing career and family. Prioritizing tasks, setting boundaries, and making time for self-care can help women manage stress and maintain their well-being.

Example: Reema, a finance manager in Chennai, created a detailed schedule that included dedicated time for work, family, and self-care activities. By prioritizing her health and well-being, Reema was able to maintain her energy levels and manage her responsibilities more effectively.

Community and Peer Support

Building a network of supportive peers and community members can provide valuable resources and emotional support for women balancing career and family. These networks can offer practical advice, share experiences, and provide encouragement.

Example: Aarti, a software engineer in Hyderabad, joined a local women's support group that focused on career and family balance. Through regular meetings and online forums, she connected with other women facing similar challenges. The group provided a platform for sharing strategies and offering mutual support, helping Aarti navigate her dual roles successfully.

Conclusion

Balancing career and family are a complex and often challenging task for women in India. However, with the right support systems, flexible work arrangements, and changing societal attitudes, it is possible to navigate these challenges effectively. By sharing real-life examples and strategies, we can inspire and empower more women to achieve financial independence while maintaining a fulfilling family life.

In the next chapter, we will explore practical strategies and resources for achieving financial independence. These strategies will provide actionable steps for women to take control of their finances and build a secure and prosperous future.

Chapter 3
Building a Strong Foundation

Achieving financial independence requires more than just desire and determination; it requires a solid foundation. This foundation is built on a clear understanding of your financial situation, setting realistic and achievable goals, and creating a budget that aligns with your aspirations and lifestyle. For Indian women, this journey also involves navigating unique societal and cultural challenges. By building a strong foundation, you can take control of your finances and pave the way towards lasting financial independence.

The Importance of Financial Education

Financial education is the cornerstone of a strong financial foundation. It empowers you to make informed decisions about saving, investing, and spending. Understanding financial concepts such as interest rates, inflation, and the importance of diversification can help you avoid common pitfalls and maximize your financial potential.

Example: Sakshi, a teacher in Jaipur, decided to educate herself about personal finance after struggling with debt. She took online courses, attended financial workshops, and read books on the subject. Her efforts paid off as she was able to pay off her debts, start saving for the future, and even invest in mutual funds. Sakshi's story highlights the transformative power of financial education.

Creating a Financial Plan

A comprehensive financial plan is essential for building a strong foundation. This plan should outline your current financial situation, your goals, and the steps you need to take to achieve those goals. It acts as a roadmap, guiding you through the various stages of your financial journey.

Example: Nandini, an entrepreneur from Bangalore, created a detailed financial plan when she started her own business. Her plan included a budget for her business expenses, a savings strategy, and an investment plan for her profits. By following her plan, Nandini was able to grow her business steadily and achieve financial stability.

Emergency Fund

An emergency fund is a crucial component of a strong financial foundation. It provides a safety net for unexpected expenses, such as medical emergencies, job loss, or urgent home repairs. Ideally, your emergency fund should cover at least three to six months' worth of living expenses.

Example: Asha, a single mother in Mumbai, set up an emergency fund after experiencing a sudden job loss. This fund allowed her to cover her living expenses and search for a new job without the stress of immediate financial pressure. Asha's experience underscores the importance of having an emergency fund.

Insurance Coverage

Insurance is another vital element of a strong financial foundation. It protects you and your family from financial hardships caused by unforeseen events. Health insurance, life insurance, and property insurance are essential types of coverage to consider.

Example: Deepa, a working professional in Delhi, invested in health insurance and life insurance policies. When she faced a medical emergency, her health insurance covered the majority of her expenses, saving her from significant financial strain. Additionally, her life insurance policy provided peace of mind, knowing her family would be financially secure if anything happened to her.

Building Credit and Managing Debt

Building good credit and managing debt responsibly are critical for long-term financial health. A strong credit history can help your secure loans with favorable terms, while excessive debt can hinder your financial progress. Strategies for managing debt include prioritizing high-interest debts, making timely payments, and avoiding unnecessary borrowing.

Example: Poonam, a software engineer in Hyderabad, used a credit card to cover her expenses during a financial crisis. However, she ensured that she made timely payments to avoid high-interest charges and maintain a good credit score. By managing her debt responsibly, Poonam was able to improve her financial situation and secure a home loan with a low-interest rate.

Investment for Growth

Investing is essential for growing your wealth and achieving financial independence. By investing in assets such as stocks, bonds, and mutual funds, you can generate additional income and build a robust financial portfolio. Diversification and regular monitoring of your investments are key strategies for successful investing.

Example: Radha, a marketing executive in Chennai, started investing in mutual funds with the help of a financial advisor. She diversified her investments across different asset classes and regularly reviewed her portfolio. Over time, her investments grew significantly, providing her with financial security and the potential for early retirement.

Building a strong financial foundation is the first step towards achieving financial independence. It requires a combination of financial education, strategic planning, and disciplined execution. By focusing on these foundational elements, you can create a solid base upon which to build your financial future.

In the next section, we will delve into the specifics of assessing your current financial situation. Understanding where you stand financially is crucial for making informed decisions and setting realistic goals. Through practical steps and real-life examples, we will guide you in taking stock of your finances and identifying areas for improvement.

Assessing Your Current Financial Situation

Before embarking on your journey towards financial independence, it's crucial to have a clear understanding of your current financial situation. This assessment provides a snapshot of where you stand financially and helps identify areas for improvement. By taking stock of your assets, liabilities, income, and expenses, you can create a realistic plan to achieve your financial goals.

Inventory of Assets and Liabilities

Start by listing all your assets and liabilities. Assets include cash, savings accounts, investments, property, and any other valuable possessions. Liabilities encompass all your debts, such as loans, credit card balances, and mortgages.

Example: Rina, a marketing professional in Delhi, created a detailed inventory of her assets and liabilities. She listed her savings, fixed deposits, and a small plot of land she owned. On the liability side, she noted her home loan and a personal loan she had taken for home renovation. This inventory helped Rina understand her net worth and prioritize debt repayment.

Tracking Income and Expenses

Maintaining a record of your monthly income and expenses is essential for financial planning. This tracking helps you understand your spending habits, identify unnecessary expenses, and ensure you are living within your means.

Example: Shalini, a teacher in Kolkata, started tracking her income and expenses using a simple spreadsheet. She recorded her salary, tutoring income, and any additional sources of income. On the expense side, she listed her rent, groceries, utilities, transportation, and entertainment. By tracking her expenses, Shalini realized she was spending too much on dining out and adjusted her budget accordingly.

Evaluating Financial Health

Assess your financial health by calculating key financial ratios, such as the debt-to-income ratio and savings rate. These ratios provide insights into your ability to manage debt and save for the future.

Debt-to-Income Ratio: This ratio measures your monthly debt payments relative to your monthly income. A lower ratio indicates better financial health.

Example: Aarti, a software engineer in Bangalore, calculated her debt-to-income ratio by dividing her monthly debt payments by her monthly income. She found that her ratio was higher than recommended, indicating that she needed to focus on paying down her debts.

Savings Rate: This ratio measures the percentage of your income that you save each month. A higher savings rate indicates a stronger financial position.

Example: Kavya, a bank employee in Chennai, aimed to save 20% of her income each month. By calculating her savings rate, she found that she was saving only 10%. Kavya decided to cut back on discretionary spending to increase her savings rate.

Identifying Financial Goals

Assessing your financial situation also involves identifying your short-term and long-term financial goals. These goals provide direction and motivation for your financial planning efforts.

Example: Maya, an artist in Jaipur, set specific financial goals such as paying off her student loan within five years, saving for a down payment on a house, and building an emergency fund. By clearly defining her goals, Maya was able to create a focused financial plan.

Reviewing Insurance Coverage

Evaluate your current insurance coverage to ensure it adequately protects you and your family. This includes health insurance, life insurance, and any other relevant policies.

Example: Neha, a freelance writer in Pune, reviewed her health and life insurance policies. She discovered that her coverage was insufficient and decided to upgrade her policies to ensure her family's financial security in case of unforeseen events.

Building an Emergency Fund

An essential part of assessing your financial situation is determining whether you have an adequate emergency fund. This fund should cover at least three to six months' worth of living expenses to protect you against unexpected financial setbacks.

Example: Priya, a single mother in Hyderabad, assessed her savings and realized she did not have an adequate emergency fund. She prioritized building this fund by setting aside a portion of her income each month until she reached her target amount.

Seeking Professional Advice

If you're unsure about how to assess your financial situation or need personalized guidance, consider seeking advice from a financial advisor. A professional can provide valuable insights and help you create a tailored financial plan.

Example: Anjali, a doctor in Mumbai, consulted a financial advisor to get a comprehensive review of her finances. The advisor helped her identify gaps in her financial planning and provided strategies to improve her financial health.

Conclusion

Assessing your current financial situation is a critical step towards building a strong financial foundation. By understanding your assets, liabilities, income, and expenses, you can make informed decisions and set realistic financial goals. This assessment provides the clarity needed to take control of your finances and work towards financial independence.

In the next section, we will explore the process of setting financial goals. Setting clear, achievable goals is essential for creating a roadmap to financial success. We will discuss how to define your goals, prioritize them, and create an actionable plan to achieve them. Through practical steps and real-life examples, we will guide you in setting the stage for a prosperous financial future.

Setting Financial Goals

Setting clear and achievable financial goals is a crucial step towards financial independence. Goals give direction to your financial planning and provide motivation to stay on track. By defining your short-term and long-term financial objectives, you can create a roadmap that guides your actions and decisions. In this section, we will explore the process of setting financial goals and provide practical steps to help you achieve them.

Defining Your Goals

The first step in setting financial goals is to clearly define what you want to achieve. Your goals should be specific, measurable, achievable, relevant, and time-bound (SMART). This approach ensures that your goals are well-defined and attainable.

Example: Suman, a marketing executive in Delhi, set a goal to save ₹10 lakh for a down payment on a house within the next five years. By specifying the amount and the time frame, Suman made her goal concrete and actionable.

Short-Term vs. Long-Term Goals

Financial goals can be categorized into short-term and long-term objectives. Short-term goals typically cover a period of one to three years, while long-term goals extend beyond three years. Balancing both types of goals is essential for comprehensive financial planning.

Example: Pooja, a graphic designer in Mumbai, identified her short-term goals as paying off her credit card debt within a year and saving ₹1 lakh for a vacation within two years. Her long-term goals included building a retirement fund and purchasing a second home.

Prioritizing Your Goals

Once you have defined your goals, prioritize them based on their importance and urgency. This prioritization helps you allocate resources and focus on achieving your most critical objectives first.

Example: Ravi and Ananya, a dual-income couple in Bangalore, prioritized building an emergency fund and paying off their student loans over saving for a new car. By focusing on their most pressing needs, they were able to achieve financial stability more quickly.

Creating an Action Plan

An actionable plan is essential for achieving your financial goals. Break down each goal into smaller, manageable steps and outline the actions you need to take. This plan should include specific milestones and deadlines to track your progress.

Example: Divya, a software developer in Chennai, created an action plan to save for her children's education. She identified the total amount needed, set monthly savings targets, and opened a dedicated savings account. By following her plan, Divya was able to reach her savings goal systematically.

Setting Realistic Goals

It's important to set realistic and attainable goals. Overly ambitious goals can lead to frustration and disappointment, while achievable goals provide a sense of accomplishment and motivation to keep going.

Example: Amit, a teacher in Kolkata, initially set a goal to save ₹50,000 every month. However, after reviewing his budget, he realized this amount was unrealistic given his income and expenses. Amit adjusted his goal to save ₹20,000 monthly, which was more manageable and achievable.

Monitoring and Adjusting Goals

Regularly reviewing and adjusting your goals is essential to stay on track. Life circumstances, financial situations, and priorities can change, and your goals should reflect these changes. Monitoring your progress allows you to make necessary adjustments and stay focused on your objectives.

Example: Nisha, a freelance writer in Pune, reviewed her financial goals every six months. When she received a significant freelance project, she adjusted her savings goals to take advantage of the increased income. Conversely, during slower months, she adjusted her goals to account for reduced earnings.

Celebrating Milestones

Achieving financial goals can be a long journey, so it's important to celebrate milestones along the way. Recognizing your progress and rewarding yourself for achieving intermediate goals can provide motivation and reinforce positive financial habits.

Example: Vikram and Priya, a young couple in Hyderabad, celebrated small milestones such as paying off a credit card or reaching a savings target. They treated themselves to a nice dinner or a weekend getaway, which kept them motivated and committed to their long-term financial goals.

Seeking Professional Guidance

If you're unsure about setting and achieving your financial goals, consider seeking advice from a financial advisor. A professional can provide personalized guidance, help you create a realistic plan, and offer strategies to optimize your financial outcomes.

Example: Arjun, a business owner in Ahmedabad, consulted a financial advisor to help him set and achieve his financial goals. The advisor provided insights into investment strategies, tax planning, and retirement savings, enabling Arjun to make informed decisions and stay on track.

Conclusion

Setting financial goals is a vital step towards achieving financial independence. By defining, prioritizing, and creating an action plan for your goals, you can take control of your financial future. Regularly monitoring and adjusting your goals, celebrating milestones, and seeking professional guidance when needed will help you stay motivated and focused on your journey.

In the next section, we will discuss creating a budget that works for you. A well-crafted budget is essential for managing your finances, achieving your goals, and maintaining financial stability. Through practical tips and real-life examples, we will guide you in developing a budget that aligns with your income, expenses, and financial objectives.

Creating a Budget That Works for You

A budget is a fundamental tool for achieving financial independence. It helps you manage your income, control your expenses, and allocate resources to achieve your financial goals. Creating a budget that works for you involves understanding your financial habits, setting realistic limits, and making adjustments as needed. This section will guide you through the process of developing a budget that aligns with your financial situation and goals.

Understanding Your Income and Expenses

The first step in creating a budget is to understand your income and expenses. Start by listing all sources of income, including salary, freelance work, rental income, and any other earnings. Next, track your expenses, categorizing them into fixed and variable costs.

Fixed Expenses: These are regular, recurring expenses such as rent, utilities, insurance premiums, and loan payments.

Variable Expenses: These include discretionary spending such as groceries, dining out, entertainment, and clothing.

Example: Meera, a nurse in Mumbai, listed her monthly income and categorized her expenses into fixed (rent, transportation, and utility bills) and variable (groceries, eating out, and entertainment). This exercise gave her a clear picture of her spending habits and areas where she could cut back.

Setting Budgeting Goals

Set clear budgeting goals based on your financial objectives. This could include saving a specific amount each month, reducing discretionary spending, or allocating more funds towards debt repayment. Your budgeting goals should align with your overall financial goals.

Example: Raj and Shweta, a married couple in Bangalore, set a goal to save ₹15,000 each month towards buying a new car. They reviewed their budget to identify areas where they could reduce expenses, such as cutting down on dining out and entertainment.

Choosing a Budgeting Method

There are several budgeting methods to choose from, depending on your preferences and financial situation. Some popular methods include:

Zero-Based Budgeting: Assign every rupee of your income to specific expenses, savings, or debt payments, ensuring that your income minus expenses equals zero.

Example: Anjali, a software developer in Chennai, used zero-based budgeting to allocate her income towards different categories. She assigned specific amounts to rent, groceries, savings, and discretionary spending, ensuring that every rupee had a purpose.

50/30/20 Budgeting: Allocate 50% of your income to needs (essentials), 30% to wants (discretionary spending), and 20% to savings and debt repayment.

Example: Amit, a sales executive in Delhi, followed the 50/30/20 rule. He allocated 50% of his income to needs such as rent and groceries, 30% to wants like dining out and entertainment, and 20% to savings and paying off his credit card debt.

Envelope System: Use cash for different spending categories and place the cash in separate envelopes. Once the cash in an envelope is used up, you cannot spend any more in that category until the next budgeting period.

Example: Sneha, a homemaker in Hyderabad, used the envelope system for her household budget. She allocated cash for groceries, utilities, and entertainment in separate envelopes. This system helped her control her spending and stick to her budget.

Tracking Your Spending

Regularly tracking your spending is essential to ensure you stay within your budget. Use budgeting tools, apps, or spreadsheets to record your expenses and compare them against your budgeted amounts. This practice helps identify any deviations and make necessary adjustments.

Example: Kavita, an HR manager in Pune, used a budgeting app to track her expenses. The app provided real-time updates on her spending and alerted her when she was nearing her budget limits. By tracking her expenses, Kavita was able to stay on top of her finances and avoid overspending.

Adjusting Your Budget

Your budget should be flexible and adaptable to changing circumstances. Regularly review your budget and make adjustments as needed. This could involve reallocating funds to different categories, increasing savings contributions, or cutting back on discretionary spending.

Example: Sunil and Priya, a young couple in Chennai, reviewed their budget every three months. When Sunil received a salary hike, they decided to increase their monthly savings contributions. Similarly, during months with higher expenses, such as festivals or vacations, they adjusted their budget to accommodate the additional spending.

Building an Emergency Fund

As part of your budgeting process, prioritize building an emergency fund. Allocate a portion of your income towards this fund until it reaches an amount that covers three to six months of living expenses. An emergency fund provides a financial cushion for unexpected expenses and emergencies.

Example: Rashmi, a freelance photographer in Kolkata, set aside 10% of her monthly income towards her emergency fund. Over time, she built a fund that covered six months of living expenses, giving her peace of mind and financial security.

Including Savings and Investments

Incorporate savings and investments into your budget. Allocate a portion of your income towards long-term savings goals, such as retirement, children's education, or purchasing a home. Regularly contributing to savings and investment accounts helps build wealth and achieve financial independence.

Example: Vikas, a banker in Delhi, allocated 20% of his monthly income to various savings and investment accounts. He contributed to a retirement fund, a fixed deposit for his children's education, and a mutual fund for wealth building. By consistently saving and investing, Vikas was able to grow his wealth steadily.

Avoiding Common Budgeting Pitfalls

Be aware of common budgeting pitfalls, such as underestimating expenses, neglecting to account for irregular expenses, or failing to track spending. Stay disciplined and committed to your budgeting plan to achieve your financial goals.

Example: Lakshmi, a small business owner in Hyderabad, initially underestimated her monthly expenses. She forgot to account for irregular expenses such as annual insurance premiums and festival-related spending. By adjusting her budget to include these costs, Lakshmi was able to create a more accurate and effective budget.

Conclusion

Creating a budget that works for you is a crucial step towards financial independence. By understanding your income and expenses, setting budgeting goals, choosing a suitable budgeting method, and regularly tracking and adjusting your budget, you can take control of your finances. A well-crafted budget helps you manage your money effectively, achieve your financial goals, and build a secure and prosperous future.

In the next chapter, we will explore practical strategies for saving and investing. Saving and investing are essential components of building wealth and achieving financial independence. Through practical tips and real-life examples, we will guide you in developing a robust savings and investment plan that aligns with your financial goals.

Chapter 4
Earning Your Worth

Financial independence starts with recognizing and earning your true worth. For many women, negotiating salary and benefits, exploring diverse income streams, and advancing in their careers are essential steps toward achieving financial independence. In this chapter, we will explore these aspects and provide practical strategies to help you maximize your earnings.

Negotiating Salary and Benefits

Negotiating salary and benefits is a critical skill that can significantly impact your financial trajectory. Unfortunately, many women feel uncomfortable or unprepared to negotiate their compensation. This section will offer strategies to help you confidently negotiate your salary and benefits, ensuring you earn what you deserve.

The Importance of Negotiation

Negotiation is not just about securing a higher salary; it's about recognizing your value and advocating for yourself. Successful negotiation can lead to better job satisfaction, increased financial security, and greater career advancement opportunities.

Example: Ritu, a software engineer in Bangalore, felt she was underpaid compared to her colleagues. After researching industry standards and gathering data on average salaries for her role, she prepared a case to present to her employer. Ritu confidently negotiated a 20% salary increase and additional benefits, reflecting her true worth.

Preparing for Negotiation

Preparation is key to successful negotiation. Start by researching the average salary for your role in your industry and location. Use resources like salary surveys, industry reports, and networking with professionals in your field. Additionally, prepare a list of your accomplishments, skills, and contributions that justify your request.

Example: Priya, a marketing manager in Delhi, prepared for her salary negotiation by researching market rates and compiling a list of her achievements, such as successful campaigns and revenue growth she had contributed to. This preparation gave her the confidence and data she needed to negotiate effectively.

Timing Your Negotiation

Choosing the right time to negotiate can make a significant difference. Aim for moments when your contributions are particularly evident, such as after successfully completing a major project or during performance review periods.

Example: Ananya, a project manager in Mumbai, timed her salary negotiation to coincide with the successful delivery of a high-profile project. Her recent achievement provided a strong basis for her request, making it difficult for her employer to deny her a raise.

Framing Your Request

When negotiating, frame your request in terms of the value you bring to the organization. Highlight your accomplishments, skills, and how your work contributes to the company's goals. Use positive language and focus on mutual benefits.

Example: Neha, a sales executive in Pune, framed her salary negotiation by emphasizing the increase in sales and new clients she had brought to the company. She presented her request as a fair compensation for her contributions and an investment in retaining top talent.

Considering the Whole Package

Salary is just one part of your compensation. Consider negotiating for additional benefits such as health insurance, retirement contributions, flexible work hours, professional development opportunities, or stock options. A comprehensive benefits package can add significant value to your overall compensation.

Example: Sonal, an HR professional in Hyderabad, negotiated not only for a higher salary but also for additional vacation days and a flexible work-from-home arrangement. These benefits improved her work-life balance and overall job satisfaction.

Practicing Your Negotiation

Practice your negotiation with a trusted friend or mentor. Role-playing different scenarios can help you anticipate objections and refine your responses. Practicing will also build your confidence and improve your negotiation skills.

Example: Megha, a graphic designer in Chennai, practiced her salary negotiation with a mentor who provided feedback and guidance. This practice helped her navigate the actual negotiation smoothly and confidently.

Staying Professional and Positive

Maintain a professional and positive attitude throughout the negotiation process. Even if your initial request is denied, express your appreciation for the consideration and ask for feedback on how you can work towards achieving your desired compensation in the future.

Example: Pooja, a teacher in Kolkata, remained professional and positive during her negotiation, even when her initial request was not fully met. She asked for feedback and agreed on a performance review in six months to revisit the discussion, demonstrating her commitment and professionalism.

Understanding When to Walk Away

In some cases, you may need to consider walking away if your employer is unwilling to meet your reasonable compensation expectations. Knowing your worth means recognizing when it's time to explore other opportunities that value your skills and contributions appropriately.

Example: Swati, a finance analyst in Mumbai, realized her employer was not willing to offer competitive compensation despite her consistent high performance. She decided to explore other job opportunities and eventually secured a position with a higher salary and better benefits at a different company.

Conclusion

Negotiating salary and benefits is a vital skill for achieving financial independence. By preparing thoroughly, timing your negotiation strategically, framing your request effectively, and considering the whole compensation package, you can confidently advocate for your worth. Remember, successful negotiation is about recognizing your value and ensuring that your compensation reflects your contributions.

In the next section, we will explore diverse income streams and how they can enhance your financial stability and growth. Diversifying your income sources is a powerful strategy for building wealth and achieving financial independence.

Exploring Diverse Income Streams

In today's dynamic economy, relying solely on a single source of income can be risky. Diversifying your income streams can provide financial security, increase your wealth, and offer a safety net during unexpected situations. This section will explore various ways to create additional income streams, enabling you to achieve greater financial independence.

The Importance of Multiple Income Streams

Having multiple income streams reduces financial dependency on a single source. It allows you to explore your interests, leverage your skills, and potentially turn hobbies into profitable ventures. Multiple income streams can also accelerate your financial goals, such as saving for a major purchase, investing, or paying off debt.

Example: Suman, a teacher in Delhi, supplemented her salary by offering private tutoring sessions. This additional income helped her save for her children's education and invest in mutual funds, enhancing her financial stability.

Side Hustles and Freelancing

Side hustles and freelancing offer flexible opportunities to earn extra income. You can leverage your skills and interests to provide services or create products that people need. Popular side hustles include freelance writing, graphic design, tutoring, and consulting.

Example: Rina, an accountant in Mumbai, started freelancing as a financial consultant for small businesses. Her side hustle not only provided additional income but also allowed her to expand her professional network and gain valuable experience.

Starting Your Side Hustle

1. Identify Your Skills and Interests: Consider what you enjoy doing and what skills you have that other may find valuable.
2. Market Research: Analyze the demand for your services or products and understand your target audience.
3. Create a Business Plan: Outline your goals, strategies, and financial projections. A business plan will guide your efforts and help you stay organized.
4. Set Up Online Presence: Use social media, websites, and freelancing platforms to promote your side hustle and reach potential clients.
5. Manage Your Time: Balance your side hustle with your primary job to avoid burnout. Set realistic work hours and prioritize tasks.

<u>Passive Income Sources</u>

Passive income is money earned with minimal ongoing effort. It provides financial security and allows you to focus on other goals or enjoy more free time. Common passive income sources include rental properties, investments, royalties, and digital products.

Example: Anita, a software engineer in Bangalore, invested in a rental property. The rental income provided her with a steady cash flow, which she reinvested in the stock market to grow her wealth further.

Popular Passive Income Ideas

1. Rental Income: Invest in real estate properties and rent them out. Rental properties can generate a steady monthly income.
2. Dividend Stocks: Invest in dividend-paying stocks. Dividends provide regular income and can be reinvested to increase your holdings.
3. Digital Products: Create and sell e-books, online courses, or software. Digital products require initial effort but can generate ongoing income.
4. Peer-to-Peer Lending: Lend money through peer-to-peer lending platforms. You earn interest on the loans, creating passive income.

<u>Monetizing Hobbies and Talents</u>

Turning hobbies and talents into income-generating activities can be fulfilling and profitable. Whether it's art, music, writing, or crafting, there are various ways to monetize your passions.

Example: Kavita, a homemaker in Chennai, loved baking. She started a home-based bakery business, selling cakes and pastries to her local community. Her passion for baking turned into a successful side business, contributing to her household income.

Steps to Monetize Your Hobbies

1. Identify Marketable Hobbies: Consider which hobbies have commercial potential.
2. Build a Portfolio: Create samples of your work to showcase your skills to potential customers.
3. Promote Your Work: Use social media, local markets, and online platforms to reach a broader audience.
4. Offer Workshops: Share your skills by conducting workshops or classes. Teaching others can be a lucrative way to monetize your talents.

Utilizing Online Platforms

The digital age has opened up numerous opportunities to earn money online. E-commerce, content creation, and gig economy platforms provide accessible ways to generate additional income.

Example: Priya, a content writer in Pune, started a blog about sustainable living. She monetized her blog through affiliate marketing, sponsored posts, and ad revenue. Her online platform became a significant source of passive income.

Popular Online Income Streams

1. E-commerce: Sell products through online marketplaces like Amazon, Etsy, or your own website.
2. Content Creation: Start a YouTube channel, blog, or podcast. Monetize through ads, sponsorships, and merchandise.
3. Gig Economy: Join platforms like Uber, Swiggy, or Upwork to offer services on a flexible schedule.
4. Online Courses: Create and sell courses on platforms like Udemy or Teachable. Share your expertise and earn money from course sales.

Conclusion

Exploring diverse income streams is a powerful strategy for achieving financial independence. By leveraging your skills, interests, and the opportunities available in today's digital world, you can create multiple sources of income that enhance your financial security and accelerate your financial goals. In the next section, we will discuss strategies for advancing in your career, helping you to earn your worth and achieve professional success.

Advancing in Your Career

Achieving financial independence involves not only managing your finances but also actively advancing in your career. Career advancement can lead to higher income, greater job satisfaction, and more opportunities for professional growth. This section will explore strategies to help you advance in your career, from building skills and networking to seeking promotions and leadership roles.

Building and Enhancing Skills

Continuous learning and skill development are crucial for career advancement. Stay updated with industry trends, acquire new skills, and seek opportunities for professional development.

Example: Asha, a marketing professional in Hyderabad, noticed the increasing importance of digital marketing. She took online courses to enhance her skills in SEO and social media marketing, making her a valuable asset to her company and positioning herself for a promotion.

Strategies for Skill Development

1. Take Online Courses: Platforms like Coursera, Udemy, and LinkedIn Learning offer courses on a wide range of topics.
2. Attend Workshops and Seminars: Participate in industry-specific workshops and seminars to gain new insights and skills.
3. Pursue Higher Education: Consider pursuing advanced degrees or certifications relevant to your field.
4. Learn from Mentors: Seek guidance from experienced professionals who can offer advice and share their knowledge.

Networking and Building Professional Relationships

Building a strong professional network can open doors to new opportunities and provide support throughout your career. Networking helps you stay informed about industry trends, find mentors, and connect with potential employers or clients.

Example: Rohini, an IT professional in Bangalore, regularly attended tech meetups and industry conferences. Her networking efforts led to a job offer from a leading tech company, significantly advancing her career.

Effective Networking Strategies

1. Attend Industry Events: Participate in conferences, seminars, and networking events related to your field.
2. Join Professional Organizations: Become a member of industry-specific associations and groups.
3. Use social media: Leverage platforms like LinkedIn to connect with professionals in your industry.
4. Offer Help and Support: Networking is a two-way street. Offer your help and support to others in your network.

Seeking Promotions and Leadership Roles

Proactively seeking promotions and leadership roles is essential for career advancement. Demonstrate your value, express your career goals to your supervisors, and take on additional responsibilities to showcase your capabilities.

Example: Meera, an operations manager in Mumbai, consistently exceeded her performance targets and took on challenging projects. She communicated her career aspirations to her supervisor and was promoted to a senior management position within two years.

Steps to Achieve Promotions

1. Set Clear Goals: Define your career goals and create a plan to achieve them.
2. Exceed Expectations: Consistently deliver high-quality work and exceed your performance targets.
3. Communicate Ambitions: Regularly discuss your career aspirations with your supervisors and seek their feedback.
4. Take Initiative: Volunteer for challenging projects and demonstrate your leadership potential.

Developing Leadership Skills

Leadership skills are crucial for career advancement, especially if you aim to take on managerial or executive roles. Effective leaders inspire and motivate their teams, make strategic decisions, and drive organizational success.

Example: Nandini, a team leader in Pune, focused on developing her leadership skills by attending leadership workshops and seeking feedback from her team. Her efforts resulted in improved team performance and recognition from senior management.

Key Leadership Skills to Develop

1. Communication: Enhance your ability to communicate clearly and persuasively.
2. Decision-Making: Develop strong decision-making and problem-solving skills.
3. Team Management: Learn how to manage and motivate a team effectively.
4. Emotional Intelligence: Cultivate emotional intelligence to understand and manage your own emotions and those of others.

Mentorship and Career Coaching

Seeking mentorship and career coaching can provide valuable guidance and support as you advance in your career. Mentors can offer insights from their experiences, while career coaches can help you identify and achieve your career goals.

Example: Sunita, a finance professional in Chennai, sought mentorship from a senior executive in her company. The mentor's advice and support helped her navigate career challenges and secure a promotion to a leadership role.

Finding Mentors and Coaches

1. Identify Potential Mentors: Look for experienced professionals in your industry who can offer guidance.
2. Build Relationships: Establish a rapport with potential mentors by seeking their advice and showing appreciation for their guidance.
3. Seek Professional Coaches: Consider hiring a career coach to help you develop and implement a career advancement plan.

Conclusion

Advancing in your career is a key component of earning your worth and achieving financial independence. By continuously building your skills, networking effectively, seeking promotions, developing leadership abilities, and leveraging mentorship, you can achieve significant career growth. In the next section, we will explore smart saving strategies, including creating emergency funds, saving for short-term and long-term goals, and planning for retirement.

Chapter 5
Smart Saving Strategies

Smart saving strategies form the bedrock of financial independence. By saving wisely, you can create a safety net for emergencies, achieve your financial goals, and ensure a comfortable future. This chapter will guide you through the principles of effective saving, helping you develop habits and strategies that will set you on the path to financial security.

The Importance of Smart Saving

Saving money is more than just putting aside a portion of your income; it's about making intentional choices that secure your financial well-being. Smart saving involves planning, discipline, and the ability to prioritize your financial goals. Here's why it matters:

1. Financial Security: Savings provide a cushion during unforeseen circumstances, such as medical emergencies, job loss, or urgent repairs.
2. Goal Achievement: Whether it's buying a home, funding education, or going on a dream vacation, having savings helps you achieve your personal and financial goals.
3. Peace of Mind: Knowing you have money set aside reduces financial stress and anxiety, allowing you to focus on other aspects of your life.
4. Future Planning: Saving enables you to plan for the future, including retirement, ensuring you can maintain your lifestyle and enjoy your later years.

Steps to Start Saving Smartly

1. **Set Clear Goals**: Identify what you're saving for—emergencies, specific purchases, or long-term goals like retirement. Clear goals provide motivation and direction.
2. **Create a Budget**: A budget helps you track income and expenses, ensuring you live within your means and identify areas where you can cut back and save more.
3. **Pay Yourself First**: Prioritize saving by treating it as a non-negotiable expense. Set aside a portion of your income for savings before spending on other needs.
4. **Automate Savings**: Automating your savings can ensure consistency and remove the temptation to spend money earmarked for saving.
5. **Reduce Unnecessary Expenses**: Identify and cut down on non-essential expenses. Small savings can add up over time, contributing significantly to your overall savings.

Example: Sneha, a young professional in Kolkata, started saving 20% of her income right from her first job. By automating her savings and sticking to a budget, she was able to build a substantial emergency fund, save for a down payment on a house, and plan for her future.

Conclusion

Smart saving strategies are essential for achieving financial independence. By setting clear goals, creating a budget, prioritizing savings, and cutting unnecessary expenses, you can build a strong financial foundation. In the next section, we will delve into the importance of emergency funds and how to create and maintain them effectively.

Emergency Funds: Your Safety Net

An emergency fund is a critical component of financial security, providing a financial cushion during unexpected situations. Whether it's a medical emergency, job loss, or urgent home repair, an emergency fund ensures you can handle unforeseen expenses without falling into debt or disrupting your long-term financial goals.

Why an Emergency Fund is Essential

- **Financial Security:** Life is unpredictable, and emergencies can happen at any time. An emergency fund gives you the financial security to manage these situations without stress.
- **Debt Avoidance:** Without an emergency fund, you may have to rely on credit cards or loans to cover unexpected expenses, leading to debt and interest payments.
- **Peace of Mind:** Knowing you have money set aside for emergencies reduces anxiety and helps you focus on other important aspects of your life.

Example: Aarti, a single mother in Delhi, built an emergency fund that covered six months of living expenses. When her company went through a downsizing phase, Aarti was able to manage her household expenses without panic while she looked for a new job.

Steps to Build an Emergency Fund

1. **Determine the Amount Needed**: Aim to save three to six months' worth of living expenses. Consider factors like job stability, health, and family size when deciding on the amount.

2. **Set Up a Separate Account**: Keep your emergency fund in a separate, easily accessible savings account. This prevents you from dipping into it for non-emergencies.
3. **Automate Your Savings:** Set up automatic transfers from your salary account to your emergency fund. This ensures consistent contributions without manual effort.
4. **Start Small and Build Gradually**: If saving a large amount seems overwhelming, start with smaller, manageable contributions. Gradually increase your savings as your financial situation improves.

Maintaining and Growing Your Emergency Fund

1. **Regularly Review and Adjust**: Periodically review your emergency fund to ensure it remains adequate for your needs. Adjust the amount as your expenses and financial situation change.
2. **Replenish Withdrawals Promptly:** If you need to use your emergency fund, make it a priority to replenish it as soon as possible.
3. **Avoid Using it for Non-Emergencies:** Discipline yourself to use the fund strictly for emergencies, not for regular expenses or non-urgent purchases.

Example: Suman, a software engineer in Pune, consistently reviewed her emergency fund to ensure it covered her evolving lifestyle and expenses. When her car required an unexpected major repair, she used the fund and then promptly replenished it over the following months.

Conclusion

An emergency fund is your financial safety net, providing security and peace of mind during unforeseen events. By determining the right amount, setting up a separate account, automating your savings, and maintaining the fund diligently, you can handle life's surprises without compromising your financial goals. In the next section, we will explore strategies for saving for short-term and long-term goals, helping you achieve your dreams and secure your future.

Saving for Short-term and Long-term Goals

Saving for specific goals, whether short-term or long-term, helps you stay focused and motivated. Clear goals give purpose to your saving efforts and make it easier to track progress. This section will guide you through setting and achieving both short-term and long-term financial goals.

Importance of Goal-oriented Saving

- Purpose and Motivation: Having clear goals provides motivation to save and helps you stay committed to your financial plan.
- Financial Discipline: Goal-oriented saving encourages disciplined spending and prioritizes financial needs over wants.
- Achieving Milestones: Saving for specific goals allows you to celebrate milestones and progress, boosting your confidence and financial well-being.

Example: Priya, a graphic designer in Chennai, set short-term goals to save for a new laptop and long-term goals for her wedding expenses. By creating separate savings plans for each goal, she was able to purchase her laptop within a year and gradually save for her wedding over three years.

Setting SMART Goals

- Specific: Define your goal clearly. Instead of saying "I want to save money," specify "I want to save ₹1,00,000 for a vacation."
- Measurable: Determine how much you need to save and track your progress.
- Achievable: Set realistic goals based on your income and expenses.
- Relevant: Ensure your goals align with your financial priorities and values.
- Time-bound: Set a deadline for achieving your goal.

Creating a Savings Plan

1. **Prioritize Your Goals**: List your short-term and long-term goals and prioritize them based on importance and urgency.
2. **Break Down Goals**: Divide your savings goal into manageable monthly or weekly targets.
3. **Allocate Savings**: Allocate a portion of your income to each goal. Use separate accounts or sub-accounts to track your savings for different goals.
4. **Monitor and Adjust:** Regularly review your progress and adjust your savings plan as needed.

Example: Anita, a teacher in Bangalore, wanted to save for her daughter's higher education and a family vacation. She set up two separate savings accounts and allocated a fixed percentage of her salary to each. By regularly reviewing her savings plan, she was able to adjust her contributions and stay on track.

Using Savings Tools and Accounts

- **Recurring Deposit (RD):** An RD account allows you to save a fixed amount regularly, earning interest over time.
- **Fixed Deposit (FD)**: An FD account offers higher interest rates for a lump sum amount locked in for a specified period.

- **Public Provident Fund (PPF):** A PPF account offers tax benefits and attractive interest rates, making it ideal for long-term savings.
- **Sukanya Samriddhi Yojana (SSY):** This government scheme is designed for the financial security of girl children, offering high interest rates and tax benefits.

Example: Geeta, a homemaker in Lucknow, used a combination of PPF and RD accounts to save for her son's education and her own retirement. By diversifying her savings, she maximized her returns and achieved her financial goals efficiently.

Conclusion

Saving for short-term and long-term goals is a key component of financial planning. By setting SMART goals, creating a savings plan, and using appropriate savings tools, you can achieve your financial objectives and secure your future. In the next section, we will delve into retirement planning, ensuring you can enjoy a comfortable and financially secure retirement.

Retirement Planning

Planning for retirement is essential to ensure a comfortable and secure future. It allows you to maintain your lifestyle and independence after you stop working. Starting early with retirement planning takes advantage of the power of compounding, helping you build a substantial retirement corpus over time.

Importance of Retirement Planning

- **Financial Independence:** Adequate retirement planning ensures you can maintain your lifestyle and independence without relying on others.
- **Peace of Mind**: Knowing you have a plan for retirement reduces anxiety about the future.
- **Early Start Advantage**: Starting early with retirement savings allows your money to grow through compounding, making it easier to achieve your retirement goals.

Example: Meena, a doctor in Hyderabad, started contributing to her Employee Provident Fund (EPF) and Public Provident Fund (PPF) in her late twenties. Over the years, her consistent contributions and the power of compounding helped her build a significant retirement corpus.

Steps for Effective Retirement Planning

1. **Estimate Retirement Needs**: Calculate how much you will need for a comfortable retirement. Consider factors like living expenses, healthcare, and lifestyle.

2. **Start Early:** The earlier you start saving for retirement, the more time your money has to grow through compounding.
3. **Choose the Right Retirement Accounts**: Explore options like Employee Provident Fund (EPF), Public Provident Fund (PPF), National Pension System (NPS), and other pension schemes.
4. **Diversify Investments**: Diversify your retirement portfolio across various investment options like mutual funds, stocks, and fixed deposits.
5. **Regular Contributions**: Make consistent contributions to your retirement accounts. Increase your contributions as your income grows.
6. **Monitor and Rebalance**: Regularly review your retirement portfolio and rebalance it based on your risk tolerance and financial goals.

Maximizing Retirement Benefits

1. **Employee Provident Fund (EPF):** Contribute to your EPF regularly to benefit from employer contributions and tax advantages.
2. **Public Provident Fund (PPF):** A PPF account offers attractive interest rates and tax benefits, making it an excellent long-term investment.
3. National Pension System (NPS): The NPS provides an additional avenue for retirement savings, with options to invest in equity, corporate bonds, and government securities.
4. **Gratuity and Pension Plans**: Ensure you understand the benefits and contribution requirements of any employer-sponsored gratuity or pension plans to maximize your retirement savings.

Example: Sunita, a school principal in Mumbai, diversified her retirement savings by contributing to EPF, PPF, and NPS. She also invested in mutual funds to balance her portfolio and achieve higher returns.

Tips for Retirement Planning

- **Stay Informed**: Keep yourself updated on changes in retirement schemes, tax benefits, and investment options.
- **Plan for Inflation:** Factor in inflation when estimating your retirement needs to ensure your savings maintain their purchasing power.
- **Avoid Early Withdrawals**: Resist the temptation to withdraw from your retirement savings prematurely, as it can significantly impact your long-term goals.
- **Seek Professional Advice**: Consider consulting a financial advisor to create a tailored retirement plan that aligns with your financial situation and goals.

Example: Rajeshwari, a financial analyst in Delhi, consulted a financial advisor to plan her retirement. The advisor helped her create a diversified investment portfolio and provided insights on maximizing her retirement benefits.

<u>Conclusion</u>

Effective retirement planning is crucial for ensuring a comfortable and secure future. By estimating your retirement needs, starting early, choosing the right accounts, diversifying investments, and maximizing benefits, you can build a substantial retirement corpus. In the next chapter, we will explore investing with confidence, helping you understand investment basics, find the right investment options, and overcome fears to take control of your financial growth.

Chapter 6
Investing with Confidence

Investing is a powerful tool for building wealth and achieving financial independence. While saving is crucial, investing allows your money to grow at a faster rate, helping you reach your financial goals more efficiently. This chapter will guide you through the essentials of investing, building your confidence to make informed decisions that align with your financial objectives.

The Importance of Investing

- **Wealth Accumulation**: Investing helps your money grow over time, accumulating wealth faster than traditional saving methods.
- **Beat Inflation:** Investments typically offer returns that outpace inflation, ensuring your money retains its purchasing power.
- **Achieve Financial Goals**: Strategic investments can help you achieve long-term financial goals such as buying a home, funding education, and securing retirement.
- **Diversification:** Investing in a variety of assets spreads risk and provides a balanced approach to growing your wealth.

Example: Deepa, a software engineer in Bangalore, started investing in mutual funds and stocks in her early thirties. Over time, her investments grew significantly, enabling her to purchase her dream home and create a solid retirement fund.

Steps to Start Investing with Confidence

1. **Educate Yourself**: Understanding the basics of investing is crucial. Read books, attend workshops, and follow reputable financial news sources to build your knowledge.
2. **Set Clear Goals**: Define your financial goals and investment objectives. Determine the amount you need to invest and the timeline for achieving your goals.
3. **Assess Your Risk Tolerance:** Understand your risk tolerance to choose investments that align with your comfort level. Higher-risk investments may offer higher returns, but they also come with increased volatility.
4. **Start Small**: Begin with small investments to gain experience and confidence. As you become more comfortable, gradually increase your investment amounts.
5. **Seek Professional Advice**: Consider consulting a financial advisor to help you create a personalized investment plan.

Example: Anjali, a marketing professional in Delhi, started her investment journey by educating herself about different asset classes. She set clear goals for her investments and began with small amounts in mutual funds. Over time, she diversified her portfolio with the help of a financial advisor, gaining confidence and achieving her financial targets.

Key Investment Strategies

1. **Diversification**: Spread your investments across different asset classes (stocks, bonds, real estate) to reduce risk and improve returns.
2. **Long-term Perspective**: Focus on long-term investments to ride out market fluctuations and benefit from compounding returns.
3. **Regular Contributions:** Invest regularly, even in small amounts, to build your portfolio steadily over time.
4. **Reinvest Earnings**: Reinvest dividends and interest to accelerate the growth of your investments.
5. **Stay Informed**: Keep up with market trends and economic news to make informed investment decisions.

Example: Rani, a small business owner in Pune, diversified her investments across stocks, bonds, and real estate. She adopted a long-term perspective and made regular contributions, reinvesting her earnings to maximize growth.

Conclusion

Investing with confidence is about understanding the importance of investing, educating yourself, setting clear goals, and adopting key strategies. By starting small, assessing your risk tolerance, and seeking professional advice, you can build a robust investment portfolio. In the next section, we will delve into understanding investment basics, providing you with the foundational knowledge to make informed investment decisions.

Understanding Investment Basics

Understanding the basics of investing is essential for making informed decisions and building a strong financial future. For many women, the world of investing can seem intimidating, but with the right knowledge and approach, it becomes an empowering tool for financial independence.

Why Women Should Invest

1. **Longer Lifespan**: Women tend to live longer than men, which means they need more savings to support a longer retirement.

2. **Financial Independence**: Investing provides women with the means to achieve financial independence and security, reducing reliance on others.
3. **Closing the Wealth Gap**: By investing, women can work towards closing the wealth gap and achieving financial equality.

Example: Neha, a marketing executive in Mumbai, realized the importance of investing when she started planning for her retirement. Understanding that she would need a larger corpus to sustain a longer retirement, she began educating herself about different investment options and started building her portfolio.

Key Investment Terms

- **Asset Classes**: Different types of investments, such as stocks, bonds, real estate, and mutual funds.
- **Risk and Return**: The relationship between the potential risk of an investment and the expected return. Higher risk often means higher potential returns, but also higher potential losses.
- **Diversification**: Spreading investments across different asset classes to reduce risk.
- **Compounding**: The process where the returns on an investment earn additional returns over time, leading to exponential growth.
- **Liquidity**: The ease with which an investment can be converted into cash without significantly affecting its value.

Example: Pooja, a school teacher in Jaipur, started with basic concepts like asset classes and diversification. She learned that by spreading her investments across different assets, she could minimize risk and enhance her chances of achieving steady returns.

Steps to Get Started with Investing

1. **Set Clear Goals**: Identify your financial goals, whether they are short-term (buying a car, vacation) or long-term (retirement, children's education).
2. **Create a Budget**: Understand your income and expenses to determine how much you can invest regularly without straining your finances.
3. **Choose the Right Investment Account:** Depending on your goals and risk tolerance, choose suitable investment accounts like mutual funds, stocks, or retirement accounts.
4. **Start Small**: Begin with small investments to gain experience and confidence. You can increase your investments as you become more comfortable.
5. **Educate Yourself**: Continuously educate yourself about different investment options and strategies. Attend workshops, read books, and follow financial news.

Example: Radhika, a software developer in Bangalore, set clear financial goals for her daughter's education and her own retirement. She started with a small investment in a mutual fund and gradually expanded her portfolio as she gained more knowledge and confidence.

Common Investment Options

- **Mutual Funds**: Pooled investment vehicles that invest in a diversified portfolio of stocks, bonds, or other assets.
- **Stocks**: Shares of ownership in a company. Stocks can offer high returns but come with higher risk.
- **Bonds**: Debt instruments where you lend money to a company or government in exchange for periodic interest payments and the return of the principal at maturity.
- **Real Estate:** Property investments that can provide rental income and potential appreciation in value.
- **Public Provident Fund (PPF):** A government-backed savings scheme offering attractive interest rates and tax benefits.

Example: Lakshmi, a banker in Chennai, diversified her investments by putting money into mutual funds, stocks, and a PPF account. This approach allowed her to balance risk and return, securing her financial future.

Conclusion

Understanding investment basics is crucial for women to make informed decisions and build a secure financial future. By setting clear goals, creating a budget, choosing the right investment accounts, and educating themselves, women can confidently navigate the world of investing. In the next section, we will explore finding the right investment options for you, helping you tailor your investment strategy to your specific needs and goals.

Finding the Right Investment Options for You

Choosing the right investment options tailored to your needs, goals, and risk tolerance is essential for building a successful investment portfolio. This section will guide you through the process of selecting the best investment options that align with your financial objectives.

Assessing Your Financial Goals

- **Short-term Goals**: These are goals you want to achieve within the next few years, such as buying a new gadget, planning a vacation, or building an emergency fund.
- **Medium-term Goals**: These goals are typically 3-5 years out, such as saving for a down payment on a house, buying a car, or starting a business.
- **Long-term Goals**: These are goals that extend beyond five years, such as retirement planning, children's education, or long-term wealth building.

Example: Shweta, a graphic designer in Pune, categorized her goals into short-term (vacation), medium-term (car purchase), and long-term (retirement). This helped her identify the appropriate investment options for each time horizon.

Understanding Your Risk Tolerance

- **Conservative**: Low risk tolerance, preferring stable and low-risk investments with modest returns. Suitable for individuals who prioritize capital preservation.
- **Moderate**: Balanced risk tolerance, willing to take on some risk for better returns. Suitable for individuals who seek a mix of stability and growth.
- **Aggressive**: High risk tolerance, comfortable with high-risk investments for the potential of higher returns. Suitable for individuals with a longer time horizon and higher risk appetite.

Example: Meera, an architect in Ahmedabad, assessed her risk tolerance and found she was a moderate investor. She balanced her portfolio with a mix of mutual funds and fixed deposits, ensuring a blend of growth and stability.

Selecting the Right Investment Options

- **Fixed Deposits (FDs):** Suitable for conservative investors looking for stable returns with minimal risk.
- **Recurring Deposits (RDs):** Ideal for regular savers who want to build a corpus over time with fixed monthly contributions.
- **Public Provident Fund (PPF):** A long-term, government-backed savings scheme offering attractive interest rates and tax benefits. Suitable for conservative to moderate investors.
- **Mutual Funds:** Diversified investment options suitable for all risk profiles. Equity mutual funds for aggressive investors, debt mutual funds for conservative investors, and balanced funds for moderate investors.
- **Stocks**: High-risk, high-return investments suitable for aggressive investors with a long-term perspective.
- **Real Estate**: Suitable for moderate to aggressive investors looking for rental income and capital appreciation.
- **National Pension System (NPS):** A retirement-focused investment with tax benefits, suitable for long-term, conservative to moderate investors.

Example: Radha, a teacher in Chennai, diversified her investments across PPF for long-term savings, mutual funds for moderate returns, and stocks for high growth. This mix aligned with her balanced risk tolerance and long-term financial goals.

Creating a Diversified Portfolio

1. **Diversification:** Spread your investments across different asset classes to minimize risk and enhance returns.
2. **Asset Allocation:** Allocate your investments based on your risk tolerance and financial goals. Typically, a conservative investor might have more in fixed deposits and PPF, while an aggressive investor might lean towards stocks and equity mutual funds.
3. **Regular Review and Rebalancing:** Periodically review your portfolio and rebalance it to maintain your desired asset allocation.

Example: Anita, a lawyer in Delhi, created a diversified portfolio by investing 40% in mutual funds, 30% in fixed deposits, 20% in PPF, and 10% in stocks. She reviewed her portfolio annually and rebalanced it to align with her changing financial goals and risk tolerance.

Conclusion

Finding the right investment options requires understanding your financial goals, assessing your risk tolerance, and creating a diversified portfolio. By carefully selecting and managing your investments, you can confidently work towards achieving your financial objectives. In the next section, we will explore overcoming fear and taking control, empowering you to invest with confidence and seize financial opportunities.

Overcoming Fear and Taking Control

Investing can be intimidating, especially for women who may have faced societal pressures and financial stereotypes. However, overcoming fear and taking control of your investments is crucial for achieving financial independence. This section will provide strategies to build confidence and take charge of your financial future.

Understanding Common Fears

1. **Fear of Losing Money:** Many women fear losing their hard-earned money in investments.
2. **Lack of Knowledge:** The complexity of financial markets can make investing seem overwhelming.

3. **Risk Aversion**: A natural tendency to avoid risk can lead to missing out on growth opportunities.
4. **Societal Expectations**: Traditional roles and societal expectations can discourage women from actively managing their finances.

Example: Priya, a homemaker in Kolkata, was initially hesitant to invest due to her fear of losing money and lack of financial knowledge. She decided to educate herself and seek advice from financial experts to overcome these fears.

Strategies to Overcome Fear

1. **Educate Yourself:** Knowledge is power. Take the time to learn about different investment options, financial markets, and investment strategies. Attend workshops, read books, and follow financial news.
2. **Start Small**: Begin with small investments to gain experience and build confidence. As you become more comfortable, gradually increase your investment amounts.
3. **Seek Professional Advice**: Consult a financial advisor to help you create a personalized investment plan. Professional guidance can provide reassurance and clarity.
4. **Join Investment Communities**: Connect with other women investors through online forums, social media groups, or local investment clubs. Sharing experiences and insights can boost confidence and provide support.
5. **Focus on Long-term Goals:** Keep your long-term financial goals in mind. Understand that short-term market fluctuations are normal and that a long-term perspective can help mitigate fear.

Example: Seema, a corporate executive in Hyderabad, started small by investing in a mutual fund with the help of a financial advisor. She joined an online community of women investors, which provided her with support and encouragement. Over time, her confidence grew, and she expanded her investment portfolio.

Building Confidence in Investing

- **Set Realistic Expectations:** Understand that investing involves risks and that not all investments will perform well. Setting realistic expectations can help you stay grounded.
- **Regularly Review Your Investments:** Monitor your investment portfolio regularly to stay informed about its performance. Make adjustments as needed to align with your financial goals.
- **Celebrate Small Wins**: Acknowledge and celebrate your investment successes, no matter how small. Recognizing your achievements can boost confidence and motivate you to continue investing.

- **Learn from Mistakes**: Accept that mistakes are part of the learning process. Analyze any investment errors and use them as opportunities to improve your investment strategy.

Example: Ankita, a pharmacist in Mumbai, set realistic expectations for her investments and regularly reviewed her portfolio. She celebrated small milestones, such as reaching her first savings goal, and learned from any investment mistakes, becoming a more confident and savvy investor.

Taking Control of Your Financial Future

1. **Create a Financial Plan**: Develop a comprehensive financial plan that outlines your goals, investment strategy, and action steps. A well-defined plan provides direction and confidence.
2. **Automate Your Investments**: Set up automatic contributions to your investment accounts to ensure consistent investing without needing to remember manual transactions.
3. **Stay Informed:** Continuously educate yourself about financial markets, investment options, and economic trends. Staying informed helps you make better investment decisions.
4. **Empower Yourself**: Embrace your role as the primary decision-maker for your financial future. Take pride in your ability to manage your finances and make informed investment choices.

Example: Nisha, an entrepreneur in Jaipur, created a financial plan with clear goals and automated her investments to ensure consistent contributions. She stayed informed about market trends and took pride in her financial management skills, empowering herself to take control of her financial future.

Conclusion

Overcoming fear and taking control of your investments is essential for achieving financial independence. By educating yourself, starting small, seeking professional advice, and staying informed, you can build confidence and make empowered investment decisions. In the next chapter, we will explore managing debt effectively, providing strategies to differentiate between good and bad debt, pay off debt, and avoid common debt traps.

Chapter 7
Managing Debt Effectively

Debt can be a significant obstacle on the path to financial independence, but it can also be a useful tool when managed effectively. Understanding how to manage debt is crucial for maintaining financial health and ensuring that it supports your financial goals rather than hinders them. This chapter will guide you through strategies for managing debt effectively, empowering you to take control of your finances.

Understanding Debt

Debt is money borrowed with the expectation of repayment, typically with interest. While some debt can help achieve financial goals, other types can lead to financial strain. Understanding the nature of your debt and how to manage it is key to financial success.

Types of Debt

1. **Secured Debt**: Loans backed by collateral, such as a mortgage or car loan. If you default, the lender can seize the collateral.
2. **Unsecured Debt**: Loans not backed by collateral, such as credit card debt or personal loans. These typically have higher interest rates due to the increased risk to the lender.
3. **Revolving Debt**: Debt that allows you to borrow up to a certain limit and pay it down over time, such as credit cards.
4. **Installment Debt**: Loans with fixed payments over a set period, such as student loans or auto loans.

Example: Ritika, a teacher in Delhi, had a mix of secured debt (a home loan) and unsecured debt (credit card balances). Understanding the differences helped her prioritize which debts to tackle first.

The Impact of Debt on Financial Health

1. **Interest Costs**: High-interest debt can significantly increase the cost of borrowing and delay financial goals.
2. **Credit Score**: Managing debt responsibly impacts your credit score, which affects your ability to secure loans and favorable interest rates.
3. **Financial Stress**: Excessive debt can lead to financial stress and limit your ability to save and invest.

Example: Megha, a software engineer in Bangalore, realized that her high credit card balances were not only costing her in interest but also affecting her credit score. This awareness motivated her to create a plan to manage her debt more effectively.

Strategies for Managing Debt

1. **Create a Debt Inventory:** List all your debts, including the outstanding balance, interest rate, and minimum monthly payment for each.
2. **Prioritize High-Interest Debt:** Focus on paying off high-interest debt first to reduce overall interest costs.
3. **Make More than the Minimum Payment:** Paying more than the minimum helps reduce the principal faster and saves on interest.
4. **Consolidate Debt:** Consider consolidating high-interest debt into a single loan with a lower interest rate.
5. **Develop a Repayment Plan:** Create a realistic plan to pay off your debt, including a budget that allocates funds for debt repayment.

Example: Aarti, a marketing professional in Mumbai, created a debt inventory and prioritized her credit card debt due to its high interest rate. She made more than the minimum payments and gradually reduced her debt burden.

Benefits of Effective Debt Management

- **Reduced Financial Stress:** Managing debt effectively reduces financial stress and improves overall financial well-being.
- **Improved Credit Score:** Responsible debt management improves your credit score, making it easier to obtain loans with favorable terms.
- **Increased Savings and Investment:** With less money going towards debt repayment, you can allocate more towards savings and investments.
- **Financial Freedom:** Managing and reducing debt brings you closer to financial independence and freedom.

Example: Kavita, an entrepreneur in Hyderabad, managed her business loans effectively, which improved her credit score and allowed her to secure additional funding for business expansion. This led to increased business growth and financial stability.

Conclusion

Managing debt effectively is crucial for financial health and achieving financial independence. By understanding your debt, prioritizing high-interest debt, making more than minimum payments, consolidating debt, and developing a repayment plan, you can take control of your financial future. In the next section, we will explore the concept of good debt vs. bad debt, helping you make informed decisions about borrowing.

Good Debt vs. Bad Debt

Not all debt is created equal. Understanding the difference between good debt and bad debt is essential for making informed borrowing decisions that support your financial goals. This section will help you distinguish between the two and guide you on how to leverage good debt while avoiding or managing bad debt.

Good Debt

Good debt is borrowing that is used to finance investments that will increase in value or generate long-term income. This type of debt typically has a clear purpose and provides a return on investment that outweighs the cost of the debt.

Characteristics of Good Debt

- **Appreciating Assets:** Debt used to purchase assets that are likely to increase in value over time.
- **Income Generation:** Debt that helps generate future income, such as education or business loans.
- **Low-Interest Rates:** Typically comes with lower interest rates compared to bad debt.

Examples of Good Debt

- **Mortgage:** Buying a home is considered good debt because real estate generally appreciates in value over time. Owning a home can also save money compared to renting in the long run. Example: Suman, a bank employee in Chennai, took a home loan to buy a house in a developing area. Over the years, the value of her home appreciated, and she built substantial equity.
- **Education Loans**: Investing in education can lead to better job opportunities and higher income potential, making it a worthwhile debt. Example: Ayesha, a student from Hyderabad, took an education loan to complete her engineering degree. After graduation, she secured a high-paying job that enabled her to pay off the loan and achieve financial stability.
- **Business Loans:** Borrowing to start or expand a business can generate future profits and create financial growth. Example: Neha, an entrepreneur in Mumbai,

took a business loan to expand her boutique. The investment paid off as her business grew, increasing her income and allowing her to repay the loan comfortably.

Bad Debt

Bad debt is borrowing that does not generate future income or increase in value. This type of debt is often used to purchase depreciating assets or for consumption that does not provide long-term benefits.

Characteristics of Bad Debt

- Depreciating Assets: Debt used to purchase items that lose value over time.
- High-Interest Rates: Often comes with higher interest rates, making it more expensive to repay.
- Non-Essential Spending: Typically associated with non-essential or discretionary spending.

Examples of Bad Debt

- **Credit Card Debt:** High-interest debt used for consumption, such as shopping, dining out, or vacations. It can quickly accumulate and become difficult to repay. Example: Pooja, a teacher in Delhi, used her credit card for frequent shopping sprees. The high interest rates on her unpaid balances quickly accumulated, creating a financial burden.
- **Auto Loans**: While necessary for transportation, cars depreciate in value. Taking on excessive auto loan debt for a luxury vehicle can be considered bad debt. Example: Rajesh, a software developer in Pune, took a large loan to buy a luxury car. The car's value depreciated rapidly, and he found himself with a significant financial liability.
- **Personal Loans for Non-Essential Item**s: Borrowing for vacations, gadgets, or other non-essential items that do not provide long-term financial benefits. Example: Shalini, a marketing professional in Bangalore, took a personal loan to fund an expensive vacation. While the vacation was enjoyable, it left her with high-interest debt and no lasting financial benefit.

Strategies for Managing Good and Bad Debt

- **Leverage Good Debt Wisely**: Use good debt strategically to invest in appreciating assets or opportunities that generate future income.
- **Avoid Accumulating Bad Debt**: Limit the use of high-interest credit cards and avoid borrowing for non-essential items.
- **Pay Off Bad Debt Quickly**: Prioritize paying off bad debt to reduce financial strain and interest costs.

- **Consolidate and Refinance**: Consider consolidating high-interest debt into lower-interest loans or refinancing existing loans to reduce interest rates and monthly payments.

Example: Vandana, an IT professional in Gurgaon, carefully managed her good debt by investing in a property and furthering her education. She avoided bad debt by using her credit card only for essential purchases and paying off the balance in full each month.

Conclusion

Understanding the difference between good debt and bad debt is crucial for making informed financial decisions. By leveraging good debt wisely and avoiding or quickly repaying bad debt, you can build a strong financial foundation and work towards financial independence. In the next section, we will explore strategies for paying off debt, helping you create a plan to manage and eliminate your debt effectively.

Strategies for Paying Off Debt

Paying off debt is a critical step towards achieving financial independence. Effective debt repayment strategies can help you reduce financial stress, save on interest costs, and free up resources for savings and investments. This section will provide actionable strategies for paying off debt and regaining financial control.

Understanding Your Debt

Before you can create an effective repayment plan, it's essential to have a clear understanding of your debt. This includes knowing the total amount owed, the interest rates, and the minimum monthly payments for each debt.

Example: Priya, a working mother in Delhi, listed all her debts, including credit card balances, a personal loan, and a car loan. She noted the outstanding balances, interest rates, and minimum payments for each.

Strategies for Paying Off Debt

1. **Debt Snowball Method**
   - How It Works: Focus on paying off the smallest debt first while making minimum payments on other debts. Once the smallest debt is paid off, move on to the next smallest debt.

- Benefits: Provides a sense of accomplishment and motivation as debts are eliminated.
- Example: Anita, a schoolteacher in Jaipur, had multiple credit card debts. She used the debt snowball method to pay off her smallest credit card balance first. The progress motivated her to continue paying off her other debts.

2. Debt Avalanche Method

- How It Works: Focus on paying off the debt with the highest interest rate first while making minimum payments on other debts. Once the highest-interest debt is paid off, move on to the next highest interest rate debt.
- Benefits: Saves money on interest over time and reduces the overall cost of debt.
- Example: Ravi, an engineer in Bangalore, had a high-interest personal loan and lower-interest student loans. He used the debt avalanche method to pay off the high-interest personal loan first, saving money on interest.

3. Consolidation

- How It Works: Combine multiple debts into a single loan with a lower interest rate. This can simplify payments and reduce the overall interest paid.
- Benefits: Simplifies debt management and can reduce monthly payments.
- Example: Meera, a small business owner in Hyderabad, had several high-interest credit card debts. She consolidated them into a single personal loan with a lower interest rate, making it easier to manage her monthly payments.

4. Balance Transfer

- How It Works: Transfer high-interest credit card debt to a new credit card with a lower interest rate, often with an introductory period of low or zero interest.
- Benefits: Reduces interest costs and can accelerate debt repayment.
- Example: Suman, a software developer in Pune, transferred her high-interest credit card balance to a card with a 0% introductory interest rate for 12 months. This allowed her to pay off the debt faster without accumulating additional interest.

5. Refinancing

- How It Works: Refinance existing loans, such as a mortgage or auto loan, to obtain a lower interest rate or better terms.
- Benefits: Reduces monthly payments and overall interest costs.
- Example: Kavita, a doctor in Mumbai, refinanced her home loan to take advantage of lower interest rates. This reduced her monthly mortgage payments and saved her money on interest over the life of the loan.

6. Increasing Income
- How It Works: Find ways to increase your income, such as taking on a part-time job, freelancing, or selling unused items.
- Benefits: Provides additional funds to accelerate debt repayment.
- Example: Lakshmi, a marketing executive in Chennai, started freelancing on weekends to earn extra income. She used this additional money to pay off her student loans faster.

7. Reducing Expenses
- How It Works: Cut unnecessary expenses from your budget and redirect the savings towards debt repayment.
- Benefits: Frees up more money to pay down debt quickly.
- Example: Rekha, a homemaker in Kolkata, reviewed her family's budget and identified areas where they could cut back, such as dining out and entertainment. The savings were then used to pay off their credit card debt.

8. Seeking Professional Help
- How It Works: Consult a financial advisor or credit counselor for personalized advice and debt management strategies.
- Benefits: Provides expert guidance and support in creating a debt repayment plan.
- Example: Rajni, a nurse in Ahmedabad, sought the help of a financial advisor to create a personalized debt repayment plan. The professional advice helped her manage her debts more effectively and stay on track.

Staying Committed to Debt Repayment

1. Set Clear Goals: Define your debt repayment goals, including target dates for paying off each debt.
2. Create a Budget: Develop a realistic budget that prioritizes debt repayment while covering essential expenses.
3. Track Progress: Monitor your progress regularly and adjust your plan as needed to stay on track.
4. Celebrate Milestones: Acknowledge and celebrate when you pay off a debt, reinforcing your commitment to becoming debt-free.
5. Stay Motivated: Remind yourself of the benefits of being debt-free, such as reduced financial stress and increased financial freedom.

Example: Sunita, a bank clerk in Patna, set a goal to pay off her personal loan within two years. She created a budget, tracked her progress, and celebrated each milestone, staying motivated throughout her debt repayment journey.

Conclusion

Effective debt management is crucial for achieving financial independence. By understanding your debt, choosing the right repayment strategy, increasing your income, reducing expenses, and seeking professional help when needed, you can take control of your finances and eliminate debt. In the next section, we will discuss common debt traps and strategies to avoid them, ensuring you stay on the path to financial freedom.

Avoiding Common Debt Traps

Debt traps can derail your financial progress and make it difficult to achieve financial independence. Understanding common debt traps and how to avoid them is essential for maintaining financial health. This section will provide insights into common pitfalls and strategies to steer clear of them.

Common Debt Traps

1. **High-Interest Credit Cards**

   - **Trap**: Relying on credit cards for everyday expenses or non-essential purchases can lead to high-interest debt that accumulates quickly.

   - **Example**: *Aarti*, a young professional in Mumbai, frequently used her credit card for shopping and dining out. The high-interest rates caused her balances to grow rapidly, leading to financial stress.

2. **Payday Loans**

   - **Trap**: Payday loans offer quick cash but come with extremely high-interest rates and short repayment terms, making them difficult to repay and leading to a cycle of debt.

   - **Example**: *Manju*, a factory worker in Delhi, took a payday loan to cover an emergency expense. She struggled to repay it on time and had to take out another loan, falling into a debt trap.

3. **Borrowing from Loan Sharks**

   - **Trap**: Loan sharks charge exorbitant interest rates and use aggressive collection tactics, creating a dangerous debt cycle.

- o **Example**: *Ramesh*, a small shop owner in Hyderabad, borrowed money from a loan shark to keep his business afloat. The high-interest rates and threats from the lender made it impossible to repay the loan.

4. **Overdraft Fees**

   - o **Trap**: Regularly overdrawing your bank account can result in hefty overdraft fees, adding to your debt burden.

   - o **Example**: *Nidhi*, a teacher in Pune, frequently overdrew her account to cover bills. The accumulating fees made it harder for her to manage her finances.

5. **Unnecessary Refinancing**

   - o **Trap**: Refinancing loans for lower monthly payments without considering the total cost of the loan can lead to higher interest payments over time.

   - o **Example**: *Ravi*, a homeowner in Bangalore, refinanced his home loan to lower his monthly payments. However, the extended loan term resulted in paying more interest overall.

6. **Living Beyond Means**

   - o **Trap**: Consistently spending more than you earn leads to reliance on credit and accumulating debt.

   - o **Example**: *Sneha*, an IT professional in Chennai, enjoyed a luxurious lifestyle funded by credit cards. Her overspending habits led to mounting debt and financial instability.

Strategies to Avoid Debt Traps

1. **Create and Stick to a Budget**

   - o **Strategy**: Develop a realistic budget that aligns with your income and expenses. Track your spending and ensure you live within your means.

   - o **Example**: *Meera*, an accountant in Kolkata, created a monthly budget that included all her expenses and savings goals. Sticking to her budget helped her avoid unnecessary debt.

2. **Build an Emergency Fund**

   - o **Strategy**: Save a portion of your income to build an emergency fund that can cover unexpected expenses, reducing the need for high-interest loans.

   - o **Example**: *Sunita*, a nurse in Ahmedabad, set aside a small amount from each paycheck to build an emergency fund. This fund helped her handle car repairs without resorting to payday loans.

3. **Use Credit Cards Wisely**

   - o **Strategy**: Limit credit card use to essential purchases and pay off the balance in full each month to avoid interest charges.

   - o **Example**: *Kavita*, a marketing executive in Delhi, used her credit card only for necessary expenses and paid off the balance every month. This practice kept her out of credit card debt.

4. **Avoid Payday Loans and Loan Sharks**

   - o **Strategy**: Seek alternatives to high-interest loans, such as borrowing from family, using a credit union, or exploring government assistance programs.

   - o **Example**: *Rajesh*, a mechanic in Bangalore, borrowed money from his family instead of taking a payday loan. This helped him avoid high-interest debt and aggressive lenders.

5. **Plan for Large Expenses**

   - o **Strategy**: Save in advance for significant expenses like vacations, home repairs, or major purchases to avoid relying on credit.

   - o **Example**: *Anjali*, a software engineer in Hyderabad, planned her yearly vacation by saving a small amount each month. This allowed her to enjoy her trip without incurring debt.

6. **Educate Yourself on Financial Products**

   - o **Strategy**: Understand the terms and conditions of financial products like loans and credit cards. Avoid products with high fees and interest rates.

   - o **Example**: *Neha*, a student in Pune, researched student loans thoroughly and chose one with the lowest interest rate and favorable terms, minimizing her debt burden after graduation.

7. **Seek Professional Financial Advice**

   - o **Strategy**: Consult a financial advisor or credit counselor for personalized advice and strategies to manage and avoid debt.

   - o **Example**: *Ravi*, a small business owner in Chennai, sought help from a financial advisor to manage his business debts effectively. This professional guidance helped him stay debt-free.

Conclusion

Avoiding common debt traps is essential for maintaining financial health and achieving financial independence. By creating a budget, building an emergency fund, using credit wisely, avoiding high-interest loans, planning for large expenses, educating yourself on financial products, and seeking professional advice, you can steer clear of debt traps and stay on the path to financial freedom. In the next chapter, we will explore leveraging technology for financial growth, helping you use modern tools to enhance your financial management.

Chapter 8
Leveraging Technology for Financial Growth

In today's digital age, technology plays a crucial role in managing and growing your finances. Leveraging technological tools and resources can simplify financial tasks, provide valuable insights, and help you make informed decisions. This chapter explores how technology can be harnessed to enhance your financial growth, making it easier to achieve your financial goals.

The Impact of Technology on Personal Finance

Technology has revolutionized personal finance by making information and tools more accessible. From budgeting apps to online investment platforms, technology offers numerous ways to manage money efficiently and effectively.

Example: *Ritu*, a marketing professional in Mumbai, found it challenging to keep track of her expenses and savings. By using a budgeting app, she gained a clear understanding of her financial situation, set realistic goals, and monitored her progress.

Benefits of Using Technology for Financial Management

1. **Convenience and Accessibility**

   - **Benefit**: Financial tools and resources are available 24/7, allowing you to manage your finances anytime, anywhere.

   - **Example**: *Anil*, a software developer in Bangalore, uses an online banking app to check his account balances, transfer money, and pay bills on the go.

2. **Automation of Financial Tasks**

   - **Benefit**: Automation reduces the need for manual tracking and ensures consistency in managing finances.

   - **Example**: *Smita*, a teacher in Delhi, set up automatic transfers to her savings account every month, helping her save regularly without any extra effort.

3. **Better Financial Insights**

   - **Benefit**: Financial apps provide detailed reports and analytics, helping you understand spending patterns and identify areas for improvement.

   - **Example**: *Rajiv*, an entrepreneur in Chennai, uses an expense tracking app to analyze his monthly spending. The insights help him adjust his budget and save more.

4. **Enhanced Security**

- o **Benefit**: Modern financial tools come with robust security features, protecting your financial information and transactions.
- o **Example**: *Priya*, a banker in Pune, relies on her mobile banking app's two-factor authentication to ensure her transactions are secure.

5. **Access to a Wealth of Information**

- o **Benefit**: Technology provides access to a vast array of financial information, from educational resources to market data, enabling informed decision-making.
- o **Example**: *Vikas*, an investor in Kolkata, uses online investment platforms to research stocks and track market trends, making informed investment choices.

Challenges and Considerations

While technology offers many advantages, it's important to be aware of potential challenges and use it wisely.

1. **Data Privacy and Security**

- o **Consideration**: Ensure that the financial tools you use have strong security measures in place to protect your personal and financial information.
- o **Example**: *Sneha*, a graphic designer in Hyderabad, only uses financial apps with robust encryption and secure login features to safeguard her data.

2. **Over-Reliance on Technology**

- o **Consideration**: While technology can simplify financial management, it's essential to understand the basics of personal finance and not rely solely on tools.
- o **Example**: *Amit*, a sales executive in Gurgaon, uses budgeting apps but also keeps a manual record of his expenses to maintain a thorough understanding of his finances.

3. **Technical Issues and Accessibility**

- o **Consideration**: Be prepared for potential technical issues and ensure you have backup methods for managing your finances.
- o **Example**: *Leena*, a student in Bangalore, keeps a physical copy of her financial records in case of app malfunctions or data loss.

Conclusion

Leveraging technology for financial growth can significantly enhance your financial management, making it more convenient, efficient, and insightful. By using the right tools and resources, you can streamline your financial tasks, gain valuable insights, and make informed decisions that support your financial goals. In the next section, we will explore specific apps and tools for budgeting and saving, providing practical tips on how to integrate them into your financial routine.

Using Apps and Tools for Budgeting and Saving

In the journey towards financial independence, budgeting and saving are foundational practices. Modern technology offers a variety of apps and tools that can make these tasks easier and more effective. This section will explore popular budgeting and saving tools, their features, and how they can be integrated into your financial routine to help you manage your money better.

Popular Budgeting Apps and Tools

1. **YNAB (You Need a Budget)**

   - **Overview**: YNAB helps users allocate every dollar to a specific purpose, promoting mindful spending and saving.

   - **Features**: Goal setting, expense tracking, detailed reports, and real-time synchronization across devices.

   - **Example**: *Priya*, a young professional in Delhi, uses YNAB to allocate her monthly salary to different categories such as rent, groceries, savings, and entertainment. This helps her ensure every rupee is accounted for and aligns with her financial goals.

2. **Mint**

   - **Overview**: Mint is a free budgeting app that provides an overview of all your finances in one place.

   - **Features**: Automatic categorization of transactions, budget creation, bill reminders, and credit score monitoring.

   - **Example**: *Amit*, an IT consultant in Bangalore, uses Mint to track his expenses across multiple accounts. The app's categorization feature helps him identify areas where he can cut back and save more.

3. **PocketGuard**

   - **Overview**: PocketGuard helps users keep track of their spending and find ways to save.

   - **Features**: Income and expense tracking, personalized insights, and recommendations for saving.

- o **Example**: *Sneha*, a marketing executive in Mumbai, relies on PocketGuard to monitor her daily expenses and stay within her budget. The app's insights help her make informed decisions about her spending habits.

4. **Goodbudget**

- o **Overview**: Goodbudget is a digital envelope budgeting system that helps users allocate money for different spending categories.

- o **Features**: Envelope budgeting, expense tracking, debt management, and goal setting.

- o **Example**: *Rajiv*, a small business owner in Chennai, uses Goodbudget to allocate his monthly income into different envelopes such as business expenses, savings, and personal expenses. This method helps him manage his cash flow effectively.

5. **Wally**

- o **Overview**: Wally is a personal finance app that provides a comprehensive view of your finances.

- o **Features**: Expense tracking, budget creation, goal setting, and multi-currency support.

- o **Example**: *Meera*, a freelancer in Pune, uses Wally to track her income and expenses in both INR and USD. The app helps her maintain a balanced budget and achieve her savings goals.

Popular Saving Tools and Apps

1. **Acorns**

- o **Overview**: Acorns rounds up your everyday purchases and invests the spare change.

- o **Features**: Automatic round-ups, diversified investment portfolios, and educational content.

- o **Example**: *Ananya*, a graphic designer in Hyderabad, links her debit card to Acorns. Every time she makes a purchase, the app rounds up the amount and invests the spare change, helping her build an investment portfolio effortlessly.

2. **Chime**

- o **Overview**: Chime offers a savings account with automatic savings features.

- o **Features**: Automatic round-ups, direct deposit, and no fees.

- o **Example**: *Ravi*, a school teacher in Delhi, sets up automatic transfers from his Chime spending account to his savings account, ensuring he saves a portion of his income regularly without extra effort.

3. **Digit**

- o **Overview**: Digit analyzes your spending habits and automatically saves small amounts of money for you.

- o **Features**: Automatic savings, goal setting, and low-balance protection.

- o **Example**: *Lakshmi*, a homemaker in Bangalore, uses Digit to save for her family's vacation. The app automatically transfers small amounts from her checking account to her savings account, helping her reach her goal without feeling the pinch.

4. **Qapital**

- o **Overview**: Qapital helps users save money towards specific goals through customizable rules.

- o **Features**: Goal-based savings, customizable rules, and joint accounts.

- o **Example**: *Kavita* and *Arjun*, a couple in Mumbai, use Qapital to save for their wedding. They set up a rule to save ₹500 every time they dine out, helping them reach their savings target in a fun and manageable way.

5. **Stash**

- o **Overview**: Stash combines saving and investing, helping users build wealth over time.

- o **Features**: Investment options, educational content, and retirement accounts.

- o **Example**: *Nisha*, a young professional in Kolkata, uses Stash to invest in a diversified portfolio while also setting aside money for short-term goals. The app's educational resources help her make informed investment decisions.

Tips for Integrating Technology into Your Financial Routine

1. **Start Small and Gradually Expand**

- o **Tip**: Begin with one or two apps to avoid feeling overwhelmed. Gradually incorporate more tools as you become comfortable.

- o **Example**: *Rekha*, a journalist in Jaipur, started using a budgeting app to track her expenses. Once she got the hang of it, she added a savings app to automate her savings.

2. **Regularly Review and Adjust**

- o **Tip**: Set aside time each week or month to review your financial data and make necessary adjustments.

- o **Example**: *Arjun*, an architect in Gurgaon, reviews his budget every Sunday evening. This routine helps him stay on top of his finances and adjust his spending as needed.

3. **Set Realistic Goals**

   - o **Tip**: Use financial apps to set achievable goals and track your progress. Celebrate small victories to stay motivated.

   - o **Example**: *Pooja*, a college student in Delhi, set a goal to save ₹10,000 in six months. She used a savings app to track her progress and celebrated every milestone, keeping her motivated to reach her target.

4. **Stay Informed**

   - o **Tip**: Use educational resources within financial apps to enhance your financial literacy and make better decisions.

   - o **Example**: *Vikram*, an engineer in Bangalore, uses the educational content in his investment app to learn about different investment options, helping him make informed choices for his portfolio.

5. **Ensure Security**

   - o **Tip**: Choose apps with strong security features and regularly update passwords to protect your financial information.

   - o **Example**: *Neha*, a doctor in Hyderabad, ensures all her financial apps have two-factor authentication enabled and updates her passwords regularly to keep her data secure.

Conclusion

Incorporating technology into your financial management can significantly simplify and enhance your budgeting and saving efforts. By using the right apps and tools, you can gain better control over your finances, achieve your financial goals more efficiently, and build a solid foundation for financial independence. In the next section, we will explore online investment platforms, providing insights into how you can leverage these tools to grow your wealth and secure your financial future.

Exploring Online Investment Platforms

Investing is a crucial step towards achieving financial independence, and online investment platforms have made it more accessible than ever. These platforms provide a user-friendly interface, educational resources, and tools to help you make informed investment decisions. This section will explore popular online investment platforms, their features, and how women can utilize them to grow their wealth and secure their financial future.

Popular Online Investment Platforms

1. **Zerodha**

   - **Overview**: Zerodha is one of India's largest and most popular online discount brokerage firms, offering low-cost trading and investment options.

   - **Features**: Stock trading, mutual funds, bonds, derivatives, comprehensive research tools, and educational resources.

   - **Example**: *Neha*, an IT professional in Bangalore, uses Zerodha to invest in stocks and mutual funds. The platform's low fees and extensive research tools help her make informed decisions and maximize her returns.

2. **Groww**

   - **Overview**: Groww is an online investment platform that simplifies investing in mutual funds, stocks, and other financial products.

   - **Features**: User-friendly interface, extensive educational content, direct mutual fund investments, and stock trading.

   - **Example**: *Pooja*, a marketing executive in Delhi, uses Groww to start her investment journey. The app's simplicity and educational resources empower her to make confident investment choices.

3. **Upstox**

   - **Overview**: Upstox is an online brokerage firm offering trading and investment services at competitive rates.

   - **Features**: Equity trading, mutual funds, derivatives, digital gold, and a robust mobile app for on-the-go investing.

   - **Example**: *Aarti*, a teacher in Mumbai, uses Upstox to invest in digital gold and mutual funds. The platform's ease of use and low transaction costs make investing accessible and affordable for her.

4. **ET Money**

   - **Overview**: ET Money is a comprehensive personal finance app that offers investment options, financial planning, and expense tracking.

   - **Features**: Direct mutual fund investments, insurance products, NPS, expense tracking, and goal-based financial planning.

- o **Example**: *Rekha*, a freelancer in Hyderabad, uses ET Money to manage her investments and track her expenses. The app's holistic approach to personal finance helps her stay organized and achieve her financial goals.

5. **Kuvera**

- o **Overview**: Kuvera is an online platform focused on goal-based investing and wealth management.

- o **Features**: Direct mutual fund investments, family account management, portfolio analysis, and tax-saving tools.

- o **Example**: *Meena*, a homemaker in Chennai, uses Kuvera to manage her family's investments. The platform's goal-based approach and portfolio analysis tools help her optimize their investments and achieve long-term financial security.

Tips for Women to Utilize Online Investment Platforms

1. **Start with Small Investments**

- o **Tip**: Begin with a small amount to familiarize yourself with the platform and build confidence in your investment decisions.

- o **Example**: *Sonal*, a graphic designer in Pune, started with a small investment in mutual funds through Groww. Gradually, as she gained more confidence and knowledge, she increased her investments.

2. **Educate Yourself**

- o **Tip**: Leverage the educational resources available on these platforms to enhance your understanding of different investment options.

- o **Example**: *Lakshmi*, an engineer in Bangalore, regularly reads the articles and watches the tutorials on Zerodha to stay informed about market trends and investment strategies.

3. **Set Clear Financial Goals**

- o **Tip**: Define your financial goals and use the goal-setting features of the platforms to plan your investments accordingly.

- o **Example**: *Ritu*, a lawyer in Delhi, set specific goals for her child's education and her retirement. She uses Kuvera's goal-based investing tools to ensure her investments align with these objectives.

4. **Diversify Your Portfolio**

- o **Tip**: Spread your investments across different asset classes to reduce risk and enhance potential returns.

- o **Example**: *Anjali*, a small business owner in Kolkata, diversifies her investments by allocating funds to stocks, mutual funds, and digital gold on Upstox, ensuring a balanced portfolio.

5. **Regularly Review and Adjust Your Portfolio**

- o **Tip**: Periodically review your investment portfolio and make adjustments based on market conditions and personal financial goals.

- o **Example**: *Shalini*, a doctor in Jaipur, reviews her portfolio on ET Money every quarter. She makes necessary adjustments to ensure her investments remain aligned with her financial objectives.

6. **Stay Informed About Market Trends**

- o **Tip**: Keep yourself updated on market trends and economic news to make informed investment decisions.

- o **Example**: *Pallavi*, a journalist in Chennai, follows financial news and market reports regularly. She uses this information to make timely and informed investment decisions on Zerodha.

Real-Life Success Stories

1. **Anu's Journey to Financial Independence**

- o **Story**: Anu, a software engineer from Hyderabad, started investing through Groww with a clear goal of buying a house. By regularly investing in mutual funds and staying informed about market trends, she was able to save enough for a down payment within five years.

2. **Divya's Diversified Portfolio**

- o **Story**: Divya, a corporate professional in Mumbai, used Zerodha to build a diversified investment portfolio. She balanced her investments across stocks, mutual funds, and bonds, achieving a healthy return on investment and securing her financial future.

3. **Meera's Retirement Plan**

- o **Story**: Meera, a school teacher from Bangalore, used ET Money to plan for her retirement. By setting clear goals and regularly investing in a mix of mutual funds and NPS, she ensured a comfortable retirement with a substantial corpus.

Conclusion

Online investment platforms have democratized investing, making it accessible and manageable for women across India. By leveraging these tools, women can take control of their financial future, make informed investment decisions, and achieve their financial goals. In the next section, we will explore strategies for managing debt effectively, providing insights into distinguishing between good and bad debt, and offering practical tips for debt repayment.

Staying Informed with Financial News and Trends

Staying informed about financial news and trends is crucial for making informed decisions and staying ahead in your financial journey. This section will explore how Indian women can stay updated with financial news, understand market trends, and leverage this knowledge to make smarter financial choices.

Importance of Staying Informed

Understanding financial news and trends allows you to:

- **Make Informed Decisions**: Stay updated on economic developments, market trends, and policy changes that may impact your investments and financial decisions.

- **Identify Opportunities**: Spot emerging trends and opportunities in various sectors that align with your financial goals.

- **Mitigate Risks**: Anticipate market movements and risks, enabling you to adjust your investment strategy accordingly.

Sources of Financial News and Information

1. **Financial Newspapers and Magazines**

    - **Examples**: *The Economic Times, Business Standard, Mint*

    - **Benefits**: These publications provide in-depth coverage of financial markets, business news, and expert analysis.

2. **Financial Websites and Portals**

    - **Examples**: *Moneycontrol, Livemint, BloombergQuint*

    - **Benefits**: Websites offer real-time updates, market data, and articles on personal finance, investments, and economic trends.

3. **Television Channels**

    - **Examples**: *CNBC-TV18, ET Now*

    - **Benefits**: Financial news channels offer live updates, expert opinions, and market analysis throughout the day.

4. **Financial Apps**

    - **Examples**: *ET Money, Moneycontrol, Bloomberg*

- o **Benefits**: Apps provide convenient access to news alerts, market trends, and portfolio tracking on your mobile device.

Tips for Staying Informed

1. **Follow Reliable Sources**: Choose reputable financial news sources and analysts known for accurate reporting and insightful analysis.

2. **Diversify Your Sources**: Get perspectives from multiple sources to gain a balanced view of financial markets and trends.

3. **Understand Market Impact**: Learn how economic news and policy changes affect different sectors and asset classes.

4. **Stay Updated Regularly**: Dedicate time each day or week to review financial news and updates to stay informed.

Incorporating Financial News into Your Strategy

1. **Investment Decision-Making**: Use insights from financial news to make informed decisions about your investments and asset allocation.

2. **Long-Term Planning**: Consider economic forecasts and trends when planning for long-term financial goals such as retirement or children's education.

3. **Risk Management**: Stay vigilant about potential risks and market fluctuations, adjusting your portfolio strategy as needed.

Real-Life Application

Case Study: Neha's Investment Journey

Neha, a software engineer in Hyderabad, regularly reads financial news on Moneycontrol and follows market updates on CNBC-TV18. She uses this information to monitor her stock investments and adjust her portfolio based on market trends. Neha credits her informed approach to financial news for helping her navigate market volatility and achieve steady investment growth.

Conclusion

Staying informed with financial news and trends empowers Indian women to make confident financial decisions, adapt to changing market conditions, and achieve their financial goals effectively. In the next section, we will explore strategies for building a supportive network that fosters financial empowerment and growth.

Chapter 9
Empowering Your Future

Empowering your future means taking charge of your financial destiny, equipping yourself with the knowledge, tools, and networks to achieve lasting financial independence. For Indian women, this journey involves overcoming cultural, societal, and economic barriers while leveraging unique opportunities. This chapter will guide you through the steps to empower yourself and others around you.

Understanding Empowerment

Financial empowerment is more than just managing money; it's about having the confidence and skills to make informed financial decisions, seize opportunities, and create a secure future. This empowerment extends beyond individual benefits, contributing to the economic growth and stability of families, communities, and society at large.

Steps to Empower Yourself

1. **Education and Continuous Learning**

   - **Importance**: Knowledge is power. The more you know about financial management, investments, and market trends, the better equipped you are to make informed decisions.

   - **Actions**: Enroll in financial literacy courses, attend workshops, read books, and follow reputable financial news sources. Utilize online platforms like Coursera, Khan Academy, and Indian financial websites for accessible learning.

2. **Setting Clear Financial Goals**

   - **Importance**: Clear, well-defined goals provide direction and motivation.

   - **Actions**: Write down your short-term and long-term financial goals. Use tools like SMART (Specific, Measurable, Achievable, Relevant, Time-bound) criteria to define them. Regularly review and adjust your goals as needed.

3. **Building a Robust Financial Plan**

   - **Importance**: A solid financial plan acts as a roadmap to your financial independence.

   - **Actions**: Create a comprehensive plan that includes budgeting, saving, investing, and debt management. Seek advice from financial advisors or use financial planning tools and apps.

4. **Investing in Your Career**

   o **Importance**: Your career is a significant source of income and personal growth.

   o **Actions**: Continuously develop your skills, seek career advancement opportunities, and negotiate for better pay and benefits. Attend industry conferences, network with professionals, and consider further education or certifications.

5. **Embracing Technology**

   o **Importance**: Technology provides tools and resources that simplify financial management and investment.

   o **Actions**: Use financial apps for budgeting, saving, and investing. Stay updated with financial news through reliable apps and websites. Participate in online communities and forums for advice and support.

6. **Building a Support Network**

   o **Importance**: A strong support network provides guidance, encouragement, and opportunities.

   o **Actions**: Connect with like-minded individuals through networking events, social media groups, and community organizations. Seek mentors who can provide valuable insights and advice.

7. **Advocating for Yourself**

   o **Importance**: Self-advocacy ensures that your needs and rights are acknowledged and respected.

   o **Actions**: Learn to negotiate effectively in both personal and professional settings. Stand up for your financial goals and don't be afraid to seek fair compensation and opportunities.

Inspiring the Next Generation

Empowering yourself is just the beginning. By mentoring and inspiring others, you create a ripple effect that benefits future generations. Here are ways to inspire and empower the next generation of financially independent women:

1. **Mentorship**

   o **Importance**: Mentors provide guidance, support, and inspiration.

   o **Actions**: Offer to mentor young women and girls in your community. Share your knowledge and experiences to help them navigate their financial journeys.

2. **Education and Advocacy**

- o **Importance**: Raising awareness about financial independence and literacy is crucial.
- o **Actions**: Organize or participate in financial literacy workshops and seminars. Advocate for financial education in schools and communities.

3. **Role Modeling**

- o **Importance**: Leading by example can have a profound impact.
- o **Actions**: Demonstrate responsible financial behavior and decision-making. Share your successes and challenges to show that financial independence is achievable.

4. **Community Involvement**

- o **Importance**: Community efforts amplify individual actions.
- o **Actions**: Join or support organizations that promote women's financial empowerment. Collaborate on initiatives that provide resources and opportunities for women.

Real-Life Stories

Anita's Journey to Financial Empowerment Anita, a teacher from Pune, transformed her financial situation through continuous learning and smart planning. She started by attending financial literacy workshops and reading extensively on personal finance. With a clear goal of securing her children's education and her retirement, she created a robust financial plan. By investing in mutual funds and leveraging online tools, Anita achieved her goals and now mentors' young women in her community.

Megha's Mentorship Impact Megha, a successful entrepreneur from Delhi, dedicates her time to mentoring young women aspiring to enter the business world. Through her guidance and support, many of her mentees have started their own ventures, contributing to a growing community of financially independent women.

Conclusion

Empowering your future involves a holistic approach that includes education, planning, networking, and advocacy. By taking proactive steps towards financial independence and inspiring others, you contribute to a stronger, more empowered society. In the next section, we will delve into the importance of building a support network and how it can significantly impact your journey to financial independence.

Building a Support Network

A robust support network can be a cornerstone of your journey to financial independence. For Indian women, creating and nurturing these networks can provide guidance, resources, and encouragement, empowering you to achieve your financial goals. This section explores how to build and leverage a strong support network.

The Importance of a Support Network

1. **Guidance and Mentorship**

   o **Benefit**: Access to experienced mentors can provide valuable insights and advice.

   o **Example**: Kavita, a marketing professional in Mumbai, credits her financial growth to the mentorship of a senior colleague who guided her through salary negotiations and investment strategies.

2. **Emotional Support**

   o **Benefit**: Emotional encouragement helps you stay motivated and resilient during challenging times.

   o **Example**: Shreya, an entrepreneur from Bangalore, relies on a close-knit group of fellow women entrepreneurs who support each other through the ups and downs of running a business.

3. **Knowledge Sharing**

   o **Benefit**: Sharing experiences and knowledge within a network enhances learning and growth.

   o **Example**: Rina, a homemaker turned investor in Kolkata, participates in a women's investment club where members share tips, strategies, and success stories.

4. **Opportunities and Resources**

   o **Benefit**: Networks can provide access to job opportunities, financial resources, and professional growth.

   o **Example**: Nisha, a software engineer in Hyderabad, found her current job through a networking event hosted by a women's tech group.

How to Build a Strong Support Network

1. **Join Professional Organizations**

   o **Action**: Become a member of professional associations relevant to your career or interests.

   o **Examples**: Women in Technology (WiT) India, Indian Women Network (IWN).

2. **Attend Networking Events**

- o **Action**: Participate in industry conferences, workshops, and seminars to meet like-minded professionals.
- o **Examples**: Annual women's leadership conferences, financial literacy workshops.

3. **Leverage social media**

- o **Action**: Use platforms like LinkedIn, Twitter, and Facebook to connect with professionals and join relevant groups.
- o **Examples**: LinkedIn groups for women in business, Facebook communities for personal finance enthusiasts.

4. **Engage in Community Activities**

- o **Action**: Get involved in community service and local organizations that align with your interests and values.
- o **Examples**: Volunteering with NGOs focused on women's empowerment, participating in community financial education programs.

5. **Seek Mentorship**

- o **Action**: Identify potential mentors in your field and build relationships with them.
- o **Examples**: Reaching out to senior colleagues for advice, joining mentorship programs offered by professional organizations.

6. **Create Support Groups**

- o **Action**: Form or join support groups with individuals who share similar goals and challenges.
- o **Examples**: Investment clubs, entrepreneurship circles, study groups for financial exams.

Real-Life Application

Case Study: Priya's Networking Success

Priya, a graphic designer from Chennai, found herself struggling with career advancement and financial planning. She decided to join a local women's business network, where she met seasoned professionals who offered mentorship and guidance. Through the network, Priya learned about freelance opportunities, investment options, and negotiation tactics. She eventually started her own design firm, leveraging the support and resources from her network to grow her business and achieve financial independence.

Case Study: Asha's Investment Club

Asha, a school teacher in Jaipur, wanted to improve her financial literacy and investment knowledge. She joined a local investment club formed by women in her community. The club members met monthly to discuss market trends, share investment tips, and review their portfolios. With the support and collective wisdom of the group, Asha confidently started investing in mutual funds and stocks, significantly improving her financial standing.

Tips for Effective Networking

1. **Be Proactive**: Take the initiative to attend events, introduce yourself to new people, and follow up on connections.

2. **Be Genuine**: Build authentic relationships based on mutual respect and shared interests rather than just transactional interactions.

3. **Offer Value**: Contribute your knowledge and skills to the network. Networking is a two-way street where giving value can lead to receiving value.

4. **Stay Connected**: Maintain regular contact with your network through meetings, emails, and social media interactions.

5. **Seek Diversity**: Build a diverse network that includes individuals from different backgrounds, industries, and expertise areas for broader perspectives and opportunities.

Overcoming Networking Challenges

1. **Overcoming Shyness**: Networking can be intimidating, especially for introverts. Start small by attending local events and gradually expand your network.

2. **Balancing Time**: Finding time for networking can be challenging. Prioritize high-value events and interactions that align with your goals.

3. **Building Trust**: Trust is crucial in any network. Be reliable, maintain confidentiality, and build relationships over time to establish trust.

Conclusion

Building a strong support network is a vital step in empowering your financial future. By surrounding yourself with mentors, peers, and resources, you gain the guidance, support, and opportunities needed to achieve financial independence. In the next section, we will explore continuous education and skill development as essential components of financial empowerment.

Educating Yourself Continuously

Continuous education is essential for maintaining and enhancing your financial knowledge and skills. For Indian women, this means staying updated with the latest financial trends, understanding new investment opportunities, and continuously improving your financial literacy. This section will explore how to keep learning and growing throughout your financial journey.

The Importance of Continuous Education

1. **Adapting to Change**: The financial world is dynamic, with new tools, policies, and opportunities emerging regularly. Staying educated helps you adapt to these changes effectively.

2. **Improving Financial Literacy**: A solid understanding of financial principles empowers you to make informed decisions and avoid common pitfalls.

3. **Boosting Confidence**: Knowledge increases confidence, enabling you to take control of your financial future and make bold, informed decisions.

4. **Expanding Opportunities**: Continuous learning can open doors to new career paths, investment opportunities, and financial strategies.

Ways to Educate Yourself Continuously

1. **Online Courses and Webinars**

   - **Action**: Enroll in online courses and webinars on personal finance, investing, and related topics.

   - **Examples**: Platforms like Coursera, Udemy, and Khan Academy offer courses on financial management, investing, and economics.

2. **Financial Books and Magazines**

   - **Action**: Read books and magazines to deepen your understanding of finance.

   - **Examples**: Books like *Rich Dad Poor Dad* by Robert Kiyosaki, *The Intelligent Investor* by Benjamin Graham, and magazines like *Forbes India* and *Outlook Money*.

3. **Podcasts and Videos**

   - **Action**: Listen to financial podcasts and watch educational videos.

   - **Examples**: Podcasts like *Paisa Vaisa* and *The Money Tree Investing Podcast*, and YouTube channels like *CA Rachana Phadke Ranade*.

4. **Workshops and Seminars**

   - **Action**: Attend workshops and seminars on financial planning and investment strategies.

   - **Examples**: Local financial planning workshops, investment seminars, and events hosted by financial institutions.

5. **Professional Certifications**

    o **Action**: Pursue professional certifications to enhance your financial expertise.

    o **Examples**: Certifications like Certified Financial Planner (CFP), Chartered Financial Analyst (CFA), and National Institute of Securities Markets (NISM) certifications.

6. **Financial Apps and Tools**

    o **Action**: Use financial apps and tools to learn and practice financial management.

    o **Examples**: Apps like ET Money, Groww, and Zerodha Varsity for investment education and tracking.

7. **Joining Financial Communities**

    o **Action**: Participate in financial communities and forums to learn from others.

    o **Examples**: Online forums like Reddit's r/India Investments, Facebook groups focused on women's financial empowerment, and local investment clubs.

Real-Life Application

Case Study: Sunita's Continuous Learning Journey

Sunita, a bank employee from Pune, realized the importance of continuous education when she wanted to start investing. She enrolled in online courses on personal finance and investing, read books like *The Richest Man in Babylon*, and joined local investment workshops. Through her dedication to learning, Sunita built a diverse investment portfolio and achieved significant financial growth.

Case Study: Divya's Professional Growth

Divya, a marketing manager in Delhi, pursued a Certified Financial Planner (CFP) certification to enhance her financial knowledge. This not only improved her personal financial management but also opened up new career opportunities in financial planning. Divya now works as a financial advisor, helping other women achieve financial independence.

Tips for Continuous Education

1. **Set Learning Goals**: Define what you want to achieve through your education, whether it's understanding a specific financial topic or acquiring a new skill.

2. **Schedule Regular Learning Time**: Dedicate a specific time each week to learning, whether through reading, attending courses, or participating in webinars.

3. **Apply What You Learn**: Practice applying new knowledge to your financial decisions and strategies to reinforce learning and see real-world results.

4. **Stay Curious**: Keep an open mind and stay curious about new financial trends, tools, and opportunities.

5. **Network with Learners**: Join study groups or online communities where you can discuss and learn from others' experiences and insights.

Conclusion

Continuous education is a lifelong journey that equips you with the tools and confidence to navigate the ever-changing financial landscape. By dedicating yourself to ongoing learning, you empower yourself to make informed decisions, seize opportunities, and achieve financial independence. In the next section, we will explore how inspiring the next generation can create a ripple effect of financial empowerment.

Inspiring the Next Generation of Financially Independent Women

Empowering yourself is a significant achievement, but the impact multiplies when you inspire and mentor the next generation. For Indian women, this involves passing on the knowledge, skills, and confidence needed to achieve financial independence. This section will explore how to effectively inspire and empower young women and girls.

The Importance of Mentorship

1. **Creating Role Models**

   o **Impact**: Young women need role models who have successfully navigated financial challenges and achieved independence.

   o **Example**: Radhika, a successful entrepreneur from Bangalore, regularly shares her journey and insights with students at local colleges, inspiring them to pursue their own financial goals.

2. **Providing Guidance**

   o **Impact**: Mentorship offers practical advice and emotional support, helping young women make informed decisions.

   o **Example**: Anjali, a financial planner in Mumbai, mentors young professionals, helping them understand investment basics and career growth strategies.

3. **Building Confidence**

   o **Impact**: Confidence is key to taking financial risks and pursuing ambitious goals.

   o **Example**: Seema, a senior executive in Delhi, runs confidence-building workshops for young women, focusing on negotiation skills and self-advocacy.

Ways to Inspire the Next Generation

1. **Becoming a Mentor**

   o **Action**: Offer your time and expertise to mentor young women in your community or industry.

   o **Examples**: Join mentorship programs, volunteer at educational institutions, or offer one-on-one mentorship sessions.

2. **Sharing Your Story**

   o **Action**: Share your financial journey, including successes and challenges, to provide real-life examples.

   o **Examples**: Write articles or blogs, participate in panel discussions, and use social media to share your experiences.

3. **Organizing Workshops and Seminars**

   o **Action**: Host workshops and seminars focused on financial literacy and career development.

   o **Examples**: Conduct sessions on budgeting, investing, and career planning in schools, colleges, and community centers.

4. **Encouraging Financial Education**

   o **Action**: Advocate for the inclusion of financial literacy programs in educational curricula.

   o **Examples**: Partner with schools to develop financial education programs, and collaborate with NGOs focused on women's empowerment.

5. **Creating Support Groups**

   o **Action**: Form or support groups where young women can discuss financial topics and share advice.

   o **Examples**: Start investment clubs, career development circles, or peer mentoring groups.

6. **Leveraging Technology**

- o **Action**: Use digital platforms to reach and inspire a broader audience.

- o **Examples**: Create online courses, host webinars, and use social media to disseminate financial knowledge.

Real-Life Application

Case Study: Neha's Mentorship Impact

Neha, a corporate lawyer in Hyderabad, mentors' young women aspiring to enter the legal field. She conducts monthly workshops on career planning, financial management, and personal branding. Her mentees often share how Neha's guidance helped them navigate their careers and make sound financial decisions.

Case Study: Pooja's Financial Literacy Initiative

Pooja, a banker in Chennai, started a financial literacy initiative targeting high school girls in rural areas. Through interactive sessions, she teaches them about savings, investments, and financial planning. Many of her students have gone on to pursue higher education and start their own businesses, breaking the cycle of financial dependence.

Tips for Effective Mentorship

1. **Be Accessible**: Make yourself available for regular meetings and open communication.

2. **Listen Actively**: Understand the needs, goals, and challenges of your mentees before offering advice.

3. **Encourage Independence**: Empower your mentees to make their own decisions rather than dictating solutions.

4. **Celebrate Achievements**: Acknowledge and celebrate the successes of your mentees to boost their confidence and motivation.

5. **Provide Constructive Feedback**: Offer honest, constructive feedback that helps your mentees grow and improve.

Conclusion

Inspiring the next generation of financially independent women is a powerful way to create lasting change. By sharing your knowledge, providing guidance, and offering support, you can help young women and girls navigate their financial journeys and achieve their goals. Together, we can build a future where financial independence is accessible to all women.

Chapter 10
Conclusion: Your Journey to Financial Independence

As we reach the conclusion of this book, it's time to reflect on the journey you have embarked on towards financial independence. This journey is not merely about accumulating wealth; it's about empowerment, confidence, and creating a secure future for yourself and your loved ones. For Indian women, achieving financial independence is a significant milestone that encompasses personal growth, overcoming societal barriers, and inspiring others to follow in your footsteps.

The Path You've Taken

Throughout this book, we've covered essential aspects of financial independence:

1. **Understanding Financial Independence**: Recognizing the importance of financial autonomy and its impact on your life.

2. **Facing Challenges**: Navigating the unique challenges Indian women face, from historical contexts to societal and cultural barriers.

3. **Building a Strong Foundation**: Assessing your financial situation, setting goals, and creating a workable budget.

4. **Earning Your Worth**: Negotiating salaries, exploring income streams, and advancing in your career.

5. **Smart Saving Strategies**: Building emergency funds, saving for goals, and planning for retirement.

6. **Investing with Confidence**: Understanding investments, finding suitable options, and overcoming fear.

7. **Managing Debt Effectively**: Differentiating between good and bad debt, and strategies for debt repayment.

8. **Leveraging Technology**: Using apps and online platforms to enhance financial growth.

9. **Empowering Your Future**: Building support networks, continuous education, and inspiring the next generation.

The Road Ahead

Your journey doesn't end here. Financial independence is an ongoing process that requires continuous learning, adapting, and growing. Here are a few steps to keep moving forward:

1. **Stay Educated**: Continue learning about new financial tools, market trends, and investment opportunities.

2. **Adapt to Changes**: Be flexible and ready to adapt to economic changes, career shifts, and personal life transitions.

3. **Set New Goals**: As you achieve your current goals, set new, ambitious ones to keep yourself motivated and focused.

4. **Give Back**: Use your knowledge and experience to help others on their financial journeys, creating a ripple effect of empowerment.

Celebrating Your Progress

In the following section, we will delve into the importance of celebrating your achievements. Recognizing and honoring your progress is crucial for maintaining motivation and building a positive mindset towards your financial journey.

Celebrating Your Progress

Achieving financial milestones, no matter how small, is a significant accomplishment that deserves recognition. Celebrating your progress not only boosts your confidence but also reinforces positive financial behaviors. This section will explore the importance of celebrating your achievements and provide practical ways to do so.

Why Celebrate Your Progress?

1. **Boosts Motivation**

   - o **Impact**: Celebrating your achievements keeps you motivated to continue working towards your financial goals.

   - o **Example**: When you reach a savings milestone, acknowledging it can encourage you to set and achieve new goals.

2. **Reinforces Positive Behavior**

   - o **Impact**: Positive reinforcement helps solidify good financial habits, making them more likely to continue.

   - o **Example**: Rewarding yourself for sticking to your budget can help you maintain disciplined spending.

3. **Builds Confidence**

   - o **Impact**: Recognizing your progress builds self-confidence and a sense of accomplishment.

   - o **Example**: Celebrating the successful negotiation of a raise can boost your confidence in your ability to advocate for yourself.

4. **Provides Perspective**

- o **Impact**: Reflecting on your achievements provides perspective on how far you've come and the progress you've made.

- o **Example**: Reviewing your financial journey can highlight the challenges you've overcome and the skills you've developed.

Practical Ways to Celebrate

1. **Share Your Success**

   - o **Action**: Share your achievements with friends, family, or a support group.

   - o **Examples**: Post about your milestone on social media, or discuss your progress at a family gathering.

2. **Reward Yourself**

   - o **Action**: Treat yourself to something special that you've been wanting.

   - o **Examples**: Buy a new book, enjoy a nice meal, or plan a short trip.

3. **Create a Visual Record**

   - o **Action**: Document your progress visually to keep yourself motivated.

   - o **Examples**: Use a journal, a vision board, or a digital app to track and celebrate your milestones.

4. **Host a Celebration**

   - o **Action**: Host a small celebration to acknowledge your achievements.

   - o **Examples**: Have a dinner party with friends, organize a family picnic, or enjoy a spa day.

5. **Reflect and Set New Goals**

   - o **Action**: Take time to reflect on your achievements and set new financial goals.

   - o **Examples**: Write a reflective journal entry, conduct a personal finance review, or set up a new savings or investment plan.

Real-Life Application

Case Study: Meera's Celebration Strategy

Meera, a software engineer in Bangalore, made it a habit to celebrate every financial milestone. When she paid off her student loans, she treated herself to a weekend getaway. When she saved her first lakh, she shared the achievement with her friends, inspiring them to set their own financial goals. This practice of celebration kept Meera motivated and focused on her long-term financial objectives.

Case Study: Anita's Visual Journey

Anita, a marketing professional in Mumbai, created a vision board to track her financial goals. She added pictures and notes for each milestone, such as buying her first car and investing in a mutual fund. Every time she reached a goal, she added a new image or note to her board. This visual representation of her journey kept Anita inspired and committed to her financial plans.

Tips for Meaningful Celebrations

1. **Make It Personal**: Choose celebrations that are meaningful and enjoyable for you.

2. **Stay Within Budget**: Ensure that your celebrations don't derail your financial plans.

3. **Involve Loved Ones**: Share your achievements with those who support and encourage you.

4. **Reflect and Plan**: Use celebrations as an opportunity to reflect on your progress and plan for future goals.

5. **Be Consistent**: Make celebration a regular part of your financial journey to maintain motivation and enthusiasm.

Conclusion

Celebrating your progress is a powerful way to stay motivated and reinforce positive financial behaviors. By recognizing your achievements, you build confidence and maintain momentum on your journey to financial independence. In the next section, we will explore strategies for staying motivated and focused as you continue to pursue your financial goals.

Staying Motivated and Focused

The journey to financial independence is long and often challenging. Staying motivated and focused is crucial to navigating this path successfully. This section provides practical strategies to maintain your drive and keep your financial goals in sight.

The Importance of Motivation and Focus

1. **Overcoming Obstacles**

   - **Impact**: Maintaining motivation helps you navigate setbacks and challenges.

   - **Example**: When faced with unexpected expenses, staying motivated ensures you stick to your budget and adjust your plans accordingly.

2. **Consistency in Habits**

   - **Impact**: Focus helps you develop and maintain good financial habits consistently.

   - **Example**: Regularly reviewing your budget and tracking expenses keeps your finances on track.

3. **Achieving Long-term Goals**

   - **Impact**: Staying focused on your long-term objectives helps you make informed decisions that align with your goals.

   - **Example**: Prioritizing savings for a down payment on a house over impulsive purchase.

4. **Building Resilience**

   - **Impact**: Motivation and focus build resilience, enabling you to handle financial stress and uncertainty.

   - **Example**: Remaining calm and proactive during economic downturns or job changes.

Strategies to Stay Motivated

1. **Set Clear and Achievable Goals**

   - **Action**: Break down your financial goals into smaller, manageable milestones.

   - **Examples**: Instead of focusing solely on saving ₹10 lakhs, aim for saving ₹1 lakh every quarter.

2. **Track Your Progress**

   - **Action**: Regularly monitor your financial progress to stay aware of your achievements.

   - **Examples**: Use a financial app or spreadsheet to track savings, investments, and expenses.

3. **Celebrate Milestones**

   - **Action**: Celebrate each milestone to reinforce your motivation.

   - **Examples**: Treat yourself to a small reward or share your success with friends and family.

4. **Stay Educated**

   - **Action**: Continuously educate yourself about personal finance to stay informed and inspired.

- o **Examples**: Read books, attend webinars, and follow financial blogs.

5. **Visualize Your Goals**

   - o **Action**: Create a vision board or use visualization techniques to keep your goals in sight.

   - o **Examples**: Place images and affirmations related to your financial goals where you can see them daily.

6. **Find a Support System**

   - o **Action**: Surround yourself with supportive friends, family, or financial mentors.

   - o **Examples**: Join a financial support group or find a mentor who can guide and motivate you.

Strategies to Stay Focused

1. **Create a Financial Plan**

   - o **Action**: Develop a comprehensive financial plan that outlines your goals and the steps to achieve them.

   - o **Examples**: Include detailed budgets, savings plans, and investment strategies in your financial plan.

2. **Limit Distractions**

   - o **Action**: Identify and minimize financial distractions that can derail your progress.

   - o **Examples**: Avoid unnecessary expenses and resist the temptation of impulse buying.

3. **Review and Adjust Regularly**

   - o **Action**: Regularly review your financial plan and adjust it based on changes in your circumstances.

   - o **Examples**: Reevaluate your budget quarterly and adjust your savings goals as needed.

4. **Practice Mindfulness**

   - o **Action**: Use mindfulness techniques to stay present and focused on your financial journey.

   - o **Examples**: Meditate, practice deep breathing, or use mindfulness apps to reduce stress and maintain focus.

5. **Stay Inspired**

- o **Action**: Keep yourself inspired by reading success stories and surrounding yourself with positive influences.

- o **Examples**: Follow inspirational financial influencers, read success stories of financially independent women, and participate in motivational events.

Real-Life Application

Case Study: Priya's Focused Approach

Priya, a graphic designer in Kolkata, set a goal to save ₹5 lakhs for her dream of starting a freelance business. She broke down her goal into smaller milestones and tracked her progress using a savings app. Priya celebrated each milestone by treating herself to a small reward, like a nice dinner. By staying focused on her plan and limiting unnecessary expenses, Priya achieved her goal within two years and successfully launched her business.

Case Study: Sita's Support System

Sita, a teacher in Pune, found it challenging to stay motivated with her financial goals. She joined a local financial support group where members shared their progress and challenges. The group meetings provided Sita with motivation, accountability, and new ideas. With the group's support, Sita paid off her credit card debt and started saving for her daughter's education.

Tips for Long-Term Motivation and Focus

1. **Revisit Your Goals**: Regularly review and update your financial goals to keep them relevant and inspiring.

2. **Stay Flexible**: Be open to adjusting your plans as circumstances change, ensuring you remain on track.

3. **Celebrate Small Wins**: Recognize and reward even the small achievements to maintain momentum.

4. **Seek Inspiration**: Continuously find new sources of inspiration, whether through reading, networking, or personal experiences.

5. **Maintain Balance**: Ensure a balance between your financial goals and personal well-being to avoid burnout.

Conclusion

Staying motivated and focused is essential to achieving and maintaining financial independence. By setting clear goals, tracking your progress, celebrating milestones, and seeking support, you can navigate the challenges and stay on course. In the final section, we will explore how to embrace your financial freedom and continue your journey with confidence.

Embracing Your Financial Freedom

As you reach the culmination of your journey to financial independence, it's time to fully embrace and celebrate the freedom and security you've worked so hard to achieve. Financial independence is not just about having money; it's about having the freedom to make choices that align with your values and goals. This final section explores how to live a life that reflects your financial freedom and how to continue empowering yourself and others.

The Meaning of Financial Freedom

1. **Empowerment**

   o **Impact**: Financial freedom empowers you to take control of your life and make decisions based on your desires and values.

   o **Example**: Deciding to pursue a passion project without worrying about financial constraints.

2. **Security**

   o **Impact**: Achieving financial independence provides a sense of security and peace of mind.

   o **Example**: Knowing you have sufficient savings to cover emergencies and future needs.

3. **Opportunity**

   o **Impact**: Financial freedom opens up opportunities for personal and professional growth.

   o **Example**: Investing in further education or starting a business.

4. **Fulfillment**

   o **Impact**: Financial independence allows you to pursue a fulfilling and meaningful life.

   o **Example**: Spending more time with family, traveling, or engaging in community service.

Celebrating Your Achievements

1. **Reflect on Your Journey**

   o **Action**: Take time to reflect on your journey and the milestones you've achieved.

   o **Example**: Write a journal entry or create a scrapbook documenting your progress.

2. **Share Your Success**

   - **Action**: Share your story with others to inspire and motivate them.

   - **Example**: Speak at community events or write a blog about your financial journey.

3. **Reward Yourself**

   - **Action**: Treat yourself to something special as a reward for your hard work.

   - **Example**: Plan a vacation, buy a meaningful item, or indulge in a favorite hobby.

4. **Express Gratitude**

   - **Action**: Express gratitude for the support and opportunities that helped you achieve financial freedom.

   - **Example**: Thank your mentors, support network, and loved ones.

Continuing Your Journey

1. **Set New Goals**

   - **Action**: Establish new financial and personal goals to continue growing and evolving.

   - **Example**: Aim for new investment targets, or plan for major life events like buying a home or starting a family.

2. **Give Back**

   - **Action**: Use your financial knowledge and resources to help others achieve their goals.

   - **Example**: Mentor young women, donate to causes you care about, or volunteer in your community.

3. **Stay Educated**

   - **Action**: Keep learning about personal finance and stay informed about economic trends.

   - **Example**: Attend financial workshops, read books, and follow financial news.

4. **Maintain Balance**

   - **Action**: Ensure a healthy balance between managing your finances and enjoying your life.

   - **Example**: Allocate time for relaxation, hobbies, and spending time with loved ones.

Real-Life Application

Case Study: Rina's Journey of Empowerment

Rina, an entrepreneur from Delhi, achieved financial independence through her successful tech startup. Reflecting on her journey, she realized the importance of sharing her knowledge. Rina started mentoring young women in her community, helping them navigate their careers and finances. She set new goals, such as expanding her business internationally and contributing to educational initiatives.

Case Study: Kavita's Celebration and Giving Back

Kavita, a doctor in Mumbai, celebrated her financial independence by taking a month-long trip to Europe, a dream she had nurtured for years. On returning, she decided to give back by offering free medical camps in rural areas. Kavita's journey inspired many in her circle to pursue their financial goals with renewed vigor.

Embracing a Life of Financial Freedom

1. **Live Authentically**: Make choices that reflect your true self and values.

2. **Stay Resilient**: Be prepared to adapt to changes and overcome challenges.

3. **Inspire Others**: Use your journey as a source of inspiration for others striving for financial independence.

4. **Enjoy the Journey**: Remember to enjoy the fruits of your labor and the freedom you've earned.

Final Thoughts

Financial independence is a powerful tool that enables you to live a life of choice, security, and fulfillment. By embracing your financial freedom, you can continue to grow, inspire others, and make a positive impact on the world. Celebrate your achievements, stay motivated, and remember that your journey is a testament to your strength and perseverance.

Thank you for embarking on this journey to financial independence. May your path be filled with continued success, empowerment, and joy.

<u>Acknowledgement</u>

This book would not have been possible without the unwavering support and encouragement of my father, Mr. V.N. Kaushik. From the very beginning, he has been my pillar of strength, always believing in my dreams and pushing me to achieve more than I ever thought possible. His wisdom, patience, and guidance have been instrumental in shaping my journey, not just as a writer, but as an individual.

Dad, this book is as much yours as it is mine. Your constant encouragement has been the driving force behind every word on these pages. I am deeply grateful for everything you have done for me. I know this book may have its imperfections, but your belief in me inspires me to continue growing and refining my craft. I dedicate this work to you with all my heart.

I would also like to extend my sincere thanks to Dr. Hiral Patel, without whom I couldn't even think about embarking on this journey. Thank you for always encouraging me and being there when I needed it most. This book wouldn't be complete without your unwavering support.

To Jenifer Aunty, I want to express my deepest gratitude. You have been a daily source of learning for me. The work you do and the encouragement you provide are beyond words. Your influence has shaped me in ways I cannot fully articulate, and I am so thankful for your presence in my life.

To my family and friends who offered their love and support during the countless hours of writing and editing, I am incredibly grateful. Your faith in me means the world, and I am fortunate to have you in my life.

Finally, to the readers of this book: your willingness to give this work a try means more than words can express. I am humbled by your support and promise to continue learning and improving in my future projects. Your feedback and encouragement are invaluable to me, and I look forward to growing together on this journey of financial empowerment.

Thank you all for being a part of this incredible journey.

Warm regards,

Shikha Kaushik

Appendix

Government Schemes

Here is a list of Indian government schemes aimed at women and women empowerment as of 2024:

Central Government Schemes

1. **Beti Bachao Beti Padhao (BBBP)**

   o **Objective**: To address the declining child sex ratio and promote the education and empowerment of the girl child.

   o **Components**: Advocacy campaigns, multi-sectoral interventions, and community mobilization.

2. **Pradhan Mantri Matru Vandana Yojana (PMMVY)**

   o **Objective**: To provide financial assistance to pregnant and lactating women to improve their health and nutrition.

   o **Components**: Cash incentives for the first childbirth.

3. **Pradhan Mantri Ujjwala Yojana (PMUY)**

   o **Objective**: To provide free LPG connections to women from below poverty line (BPL) households.

   o **Components**: Financial assistance for the purchase of LPG connections.

4. **Mahila E-Haat**

   o **Objective**: To provide an online marketing platform for women entrepreneurs to showcase their products.

   o **Components**: Digital marketing and e-commerce support.

5. **One Stop Centre Scheme (Sakhi)**

   o **Objective**: To provide integrated support and assistance to women affected by violence.

   o **Components**: Medical, legal, psychological, and counseling services.

6. **Mahila Shakti Kendra (MSK)**

   o **Objective**: To empower rural women through community participation.

- o **Components**: Capacity building and training programs at the village level.

7. **SWADHAR Greh**

   - o **Objective**: To provide shelter, food, clothing, and care to marginalized women and girls.

   - o **Components**: Shelter homes and rehabilitation services.

8. **Working Women Hostel Scheme**

   - o **Objective**: To provide safe and affordable accommodation for working women.

   - o **Components**: Hostels with daycare facilities for children.

9. **Rashtriya Mahila Kosh (RMK)**

   - o **Objective**: To provide micro-finance services to poor women.

   - o **Components**: Loans for income-generating activities.

10. **STEP (Support to Training and Employment Program for Women)**

    - o **Objective**: To provide skills that give employability to women.

    - o **Components**: Training programs in various sectors like agriculture, horticulture, food processing, etc.

11. **National Creche Scheme**

    - o **Objective**: To provide daycare facilities to children of working mothers.

    - o **Components**: Daycare services, supplementary nutrition, and healthcare services.

State Government Schemes

1. **Karnataka: Bhagyashree Scheme**

   - o **Objective**: To promote the birth of girl children in economically weaker families.

   - o **Components**: Financial assistance and insurance cover.

2. **Tamil Nadu: Amma Two-Wheeler Scheme**

   - o **Objective**: To empower working women by providing subsidized two-wheelers.

   - o **Components**: Financial subsidy for purchasing scooters.

3. **Madhya Pradesh: Ladli Laxmi Yojana**

- o **Objective**: To improve the educational and economic status of girls.

- o **Components**: Financial assistance for education and marriage.

4. **Maharashtra: Tejaswini Scheme**

    - o **Objective**: To empower women through skill development and entrepreneurship.

    - o **Components**: Training programs and financial assistance for startups.

5. **Rajasthan: Rajshree Yojana**

    - o **Objective**: To improve the health and educational status of girls.

    - o **Components**: Financial incentives from birth until the completion of schooling.

6. **Haryana: Mukhya Mantri Vivah Shagun Yojana**

    - o **Objective**: To provide financial assistance for the marriage of girls from economically weaker sections.

    - o **Components**: Cash assistance for wedding expenses.

Recent Initiatives (up to 2024)

1. **Nari Shakti Puraskar**

    - o **Objective**: To recognize and honor exceptional contributions by individuals and institutions for women's empowerment.

    - o **Components**: Awards and recognition.

2. **Women Entrepreneurship Platform (WEP)**

    - o **Objective**: To create an ecosystem for fostering entrepreneurship among women.

    - o **Components**: Support and resources for women entrepreneurs.

3. **Mahila Police Volunteers (MPVs)**

    - o **Objective**: To facilitate the outreach of police services to women.

    - o **Components**: Engagement of volunteers to report incidents of violence against women.

4. **Samarthya Scheme**

- o **Objective**: To provide vocational training and skill development to women.
- o **Components**: Training programs in various sectors to enhance employability.

5. **Women Empowerment and Livelihood Program in the Mid Gangetic Plain (WEALP)**

- o **Objective**: To improve the socio-economic status of women in rural areas.
- o **Components**: Livelihood training and financial support.

Checklist- Financially Independent

1. Understanding Financial Independence:

- Define what financial independence means to you.
- Identify your financial goals and objectives.
- Assess your current financial situation.

2. Setting Financial Goals:

- List short-term financial goals (e.g., save for a vacation, pay off a credit card).
- List long-term financial goals (e.g., buy a house, save for retirement).
- Set specific, measurable, achievable, relevant, and time-bound (SMART) goals.

3. Creating a Budget:

- Track your income and expenses for a month.
- Categorize your expenses (e.g., fixed, variable, discretionary).
- Identify areas where you can cut back.
- Allocate funds towards savings and investments.

4. Saving Strategies:

- Set up an emergency fund (3-6 months of expenses).
- Automate your savings.
- Save for specific goals (e.g., education, retirement).
- Use high-yield savings accounts.

5. Investing Basics:

- Understand different types of investments (e.g., stocks, bonds, mutual funds).
- Determine your risk tolerance.
- Diversify your investment portfolio.
- Start investing early to benefit from compounding.

6. Managing Debt:

- List all your debts with interest rates and balances.
- Prioritize paying off high-interest debt first.
- Consider debt consolidation if necessary.
- Avoid taking on new debt.

7. Using Technology for Financial Growth:

- Download budgeting apps (e.g., Mint, YNAB).
- Use investment platforms (e.g., Zerodha, Groww).
- Stay informed with financial news apps (e.g., Moneycontrol, Economic Times).

8. Building a Support Network:

- Join financial literacy groups and forums.
- Find a financial mentor or advisor.
- Attend workshops and seminars on personal finance.

Checklist - Empowerment and Personal Development

1. Building Confidence:

- Practice positive self-talk.
- Set and achieve small, incremental goals.
- Seek constructive feedback and act on it.

2. Enhancing Skills:

- Identify skills relevant to your career or business.
- Enroll in courses or workshops to improve these skills.
- Regularly update your knowledge and stay current in your field.

3. Networking:

- Join professional organizations and associations.
- Attend industry conferences and events.
- Connect with peers and mentors on LinkedIn.

4. Balancing Career and Family:

- Set clear boundaries between work and personal time.
- Plan and schedule family activities in advance.
- Communicate openly with family members about your goals and commitments.

5. Staying Motivated:

- Write down your long-term vision and revisit it regularly.
- Reward yourself for achieving milestones.
- Surround yourself with positive influences and role models.

6. Giving Back:

- Identify causes you are passionate about.
- Volunteer your time or skills to community projects.
- Mentor younger women or those just starting their financial independence journey.

Checklist - Safety and Legal Awareness

1. Legal Rights:

- Educate yourself about your legal rights as a woman in India.
- Know the laws related to domestic violence, sexual harassment, and workplace equality.

2. Safety Measures:

- Install safety apps on your phone (e.g., Raksha, Safetipin).
- Keep emergency contacts easily accessible.
- Be aware of your surroundings and avoid risky areas when possible.

3. Financial Protection:

- Keep personal and financial documents in a safe place.
- Consider getting insurance (health, life, and property).
- Monitor your credit report regularly for any discrepancies.

Checklist - Safety and Legal Awareness

Checklist - Health and Wellness

1. Physical Health:

- Schedule regular health check-ups.
- Maintain a balanced diet and stay hydrated.
- Incorporate regular physical activity into your routine.

2. Mental Health:

- Practice mindfulness and stress-relief techniques (e.g., meditation, yoga).
- Seek professional help if needed (e.g., therapy, counseling).
- Allocate time for hobbies and activities you enjoy.

3. Work-Life Balance:

- Set realistic expectations and prioritize tasks.
- Take regular breaks to avoid burnout.
- Learn to say no and delegate tasks when necessary.

Checklist - Health and Wellness

Monthly Budget Planner

MONTHLY BUDGET PLANNER

Budget Goal: _________________________   Month: _________________________

Income

Date	Description	Amount
Total		

Fixed Expenses

Date	Description	Amount
Total		

Other Expenses

Date	Description	Amount
Total		

Bills

Date	Description	Amount
Total		

Recap

	Goal	Actual	Difference
Earnt			
Spent			
Debt			
Saved			

Yearly Budget Planner

Yearly
OVERVIEW

MONTH:

MONTH	INCOME	BILLS	SAVINGS	DEBT	EXPENSES
○ JANUARY					
○ FEBRUARY					
○ MARCH					
○ APRIL					
○ MAY					
○ JUNE					
○ JULY					
○ AUGUST					
○ SEPTEMBER					
○ OCTOBER					
○ NOVEMBER					
○ DECEMBER					
TOTAL:					

RESULT

NOTES

Saving Tracker

Savings Tracker

Saving For: ___________________   **Goal Monthly Deposit:** ___________________

Amount To Save: ___________________   **Goal End Date:** ___________________

Month	Date Of Deposit	Amount Deposit	Amount Remaining

Saving Tracker

INCOME TRACKER

Month:

Date	Source	Description	Amount
		Total	

Expense Tracker

EXPENSE TRACKER

MONTH OF

DATE	DESCRIPTION	CATEGORY	AMOUNT

Expense Tracker

Debt Tracker

DEBT PAYMENT TRACKER

CREADITOR		
ACCOUNT NO:		
INTEREST RATE:		
STARTING BALANCE:		
DUE DATE:		
MONTH	**PAID**	**BALANCE**
JAN		
FEB		
MAR		
APR		
MAY		
JUN		
JUL		
AUG		
SEP		
OCT		
NOV		
DEC		

CREADITOR		
ACCOUNT NO:		
INTEREST RATE:		
STARTING BALANCE:		
DUE DATE:		
MONTH	**PAID**	**BALANCE**
JAN		
FEB		
MAR		
APR		
MAY		
JUN		
JUL		
AUG		
SEP		
OCT		
NOV		
DEC		

CREADITOR		
ACCOUNT NO:		
INTEREST RATE:		
STARTING BALANCE:		
DUE DATE:		
MONTH	**PAID**	**BALANCE**
JAN		
FEB		
MAR		
APR		
MAY		
JUN		
JUL		
AUG		
SEP		
OCT		
NOV		
DEC		

CREADITOR		
ACCOUNT NO:		
INTEREST RATE:		
STARTING BALANCE:		
DUE DATE:		
MONTH	**PAID**	**BALANCE**
JAN		
FEB		
MAR		
APR		
MAY		
JUN		
JUL		
AUG		
SEP		
OCT		
NOV		
DEC		